Peril and Promise
A Commentary on America

JOHN CHANCELLOR
Peril and Promise
A Commentary on America

1817

HARPER & ROW, PUBLISHERS, NEW YORK

GRAND RAPIDS, PHILADELPHIA, ST. LOUIS, SAN FRANCISCO
LONDON, SINGAPORE, SYDNEY, TOKYO, TORONTO

PERIL AND PROMISE: *A Commentary On* AMERICA. Copyright © 1990 by Counterpoint Communications, Inc. All rights reserved. Printed in the United States of America. No part of this book may be used or reproduced in any manner whatsoever without written permission except in the case of brief quotations embodied in critical articles and reviews. For information address Harper & Row, Publishers, Inc., 10 East 53rd Street, New York, NY 10022.

FIRST TRADE EDITION

Designed by Helene Berinsky

LIBRARY OF CONGRESS CATALOG CARD NUMBER 89-46082

ISBN 0-06-016336-4

90 91 92 93 94 CC/RRD 10 9 8 7 6 5 4 3 2 1

For Frances Lindley

CONTENTS

Prologue   11

·

PART ONE

THE INDICTMENT

13

·

PART TWO

AMERICA, 1970–90:
HOW DID A COUNTRY SO RICH
GET SO POOR?

57

·

PART THREE

HOW DO WE GET OUT OF THIS MESS?

127

·

Sources   165

Index   169

Peril and Promise

A Commentary on America

PROLOGUE

This book was written in anger and frustration in the autumn of 1989 and the winter of 1990, as the United States continued to demonstrate an inability to manage its affairs.

My anger is caused by our borrowing from foreigners to maintain what seems to me a sham prosperity; by the failure of the federal government to address America's indebtedness in an honest way; by the loss of our competitive position in the world; by the scandalous performance of the country's educational system; by the decay of our inner cities; by the beggaring of America's children; and perhaps, most of all, by the infuriating custom of our political leaders to avoid difficult decisions.

My frustration is caused by the realization that millions of Americans underestimate the enormous strength of the United States, by the fact that many appear to have given up the fight, and by the sad spectacle of an America that seems to be running out of steam.

I stand with Carl Schurz, who said, "Our country, right or wrong. When right, to be kept right; when wrong, to be put right." It is time to put America right. This country needs to build on its immense reservoir of power, to energize the talent of its people, to return to the hard work and dedication that made the United States a champion among the nations of the world.

That is what this book is about. It provides a place to stand where the strengths *and* the weaknesses can be seen. It shows how danger crept up on America. And it offers ideas on how the strength of America can be used to build a safe and successful future.

This is not a text on history or economics, although there is some of both in these pages. I am a journalist, not a historian or an economist. I see things through the lens of journalism, which often creates a picture of the world that is made up of equal parts of despair and hope.

Nor is this a book about the inevitability of the decline of America. There is a growing declinist literature, of which the most popular is Paul Kennedy's *The Rise and Fall of the Great Powers*. Mine is not a declinist argument, although I may be accused of being soft on declinism. I don't believe there are ineluctable forces pushing the United States into decline. My view is that our problems are our own fault. We created them and we can solve them.

If these problems can't be solved, I believe the country will slide downhill and perhaps never regain its primacy in world affairs. That is why there must be a restructuring of the way we manage our affairs and a rethinking of how the country operates. If these goals are achieved, there is enough vitality, intelligence, and resiliency in the American system to maintain the position of the United States. I am an optimist, not a declinist, but I am a frightened optimist.

PART ONE

The Indictment

N o country in the world has been as blessed by nature and circumstance as has the United States of America. It is a land rich in mineral wealth, its spacious plains watered by great rivers and its climate diverse and stimulating. For much of its history, it has been protected by wide oceans from the troubles of Europe and Asia.

No country in the world has had as stable a system of government for so long. Few nations have had such an inspiring birth: The infant country was shaped by the best and most sophisticated philosophers of the time. And throughout, the United States has been enriched by the largest and most productive flow of immigrants in the annals of history.

No country in the twentieth century has had such power in war and peace. The United States was the deciding force in the outcome of two world wars. Its generosity after World War II, shared by its allies and enemies alike, made possible the reconstruction of the postwar world. Its military strength shielded the democracies from tyranny and revolution while its diplomacy helped shape and sustain a system of world order in politics and commerce.

No country in the past half century has had a comparable impact on science, medicine, and the arts. American popular culture is the most influential in the world. Its medical discoveries have made the planet a healthier place. Its benevolence has given life and hope to millions in poor countries. America invented the technologies that are transforming society.

The United States has the most productive national economy in the world. In 1990, the United States was in its eighth year of economic expansion, its unemployment rate was low, and inflation was not a problem. According to the final estimate from the Central Intelligence Agency for 1988, the United States produced more goods and services than did any other country, by far. It produced more than five times as much as West Germany, the most productive country in Western Europe, and more than twice as much as Japan, the giant of the Pacific. In 1988, according to the CIA, the United States produced more than one-fourth of all the goods and services in the world. No other country comes near to matching that enormous output.

Yet there are alarming signs, as the United States moves into the final decade of the century, that things have gone badly wrong in America. The country's superiority abroad is under serious challenge, and its standard of living at home is deteriorating. Its government and trade deficits are so high that it needs enormous amounts of foreign capital—about $10 billion a month—to keep its economy alive. Its educational system is in dangerous disrepair, its population imperiled, and its cities under siege because of drugs and poverty. America's ability to compete in world markets has diminished, and the threat from Japan and Western Europe has increased.

Moreover, many Americans believe the United States has already surrendered world economic leadership to Japan, despite evidence to the contrary. A national poll of Americans by NBC News and the *Wall Street Journal* in 1990 found that only 15 percent believed that the United States was the number one economic power in the world. More than seven out of ten said Japan was in a stronger economic position. In the face of overwhelming statistical evidence of their country's economic superiority, millions of Americans had concluded that Japan was the richest country on the planet. A Harris survey showed that by a margin of two to one, Americans believe foreign companies will dominate the American economy within the next ten years.

There is serious concern that the competitive contest is being lost to the Japanese and the Europeans. Some of the anxiety is based on fact: the unquenchable American appetite for foreign products, the loss of American competitiveness overseas, the huge trade and government deficits that require foreign support. Some of the anxiety is driven by myth: the idea that some mysterious secret in the culture of Japan guarantees its economic success, that much foreign competition is unbeatable because of cheap wages, that foreign factories are newer and more productive than are American factories because they were rebuilt after the destruction of World War II. None of the latter ideas is true, but underneath these myths lies a defeatist presumption that the battle for world leadership has been lost. There is a widespread feeling that the sacrifices of World War II were in vain, that the countries that lost the war have achieved in the 1980s much of what they had not been able to accomplish in the war. West Germany has become the world's largest exporter; Japan is wealthier and more powerful than ever before.

Another reason for the underestimation of American strength can be found in the politics of the 1988 presidential campaigns. Michael Dukakis, challenging eight years of Reaganism, did not emphasize America's economic power. And George Bush, threatened by Dukakis's early popularity, spent most of his time attacking his Democratic opponent on matters that did not deal with the strength of the United States. Irrelevancies, such as the Pledge of Allegiance, the Massachusetts prison furlough program, and pollution in Boston harbor, came to dominate the campaign. Ronald Reagan had constantly emphasized that America was the world's strongest power; during the Bush campaign, the Reagan administration's slogans about America being number one were lost in a cacophony of shallow politics. And when Mr. Bush became president, his inaugural message was not about America's strength; instead, it was a signal that in his kinder, gentler America the government would not have much money to spend on solving problems. Americans, he said, had more will than wallet.

Bush was right about the slender wallet, but there is also doubt about the people's will. There is a feeling in America that something has gone seriously wrong, that old assumptions aren't reliable. For almost three decades following World War II, the quality of life and the standard of living in the United States had risen. There were recessions, strikes, and other misfortunes, but, in general, life was good; the upward trend was steady. Americans lived better and more productive lives than did their parents and believed their children would lead even better lives. By 1989, that fundamental optimism was eroding.

In that year a poll by NBC News and the *Wall Street Journal* showed that only 40 percent of those polled forecast a higher standard of living for their children. People who thought the American standard of living was falling outnumbered those who thought it was rising. (It was still rising in 1989, but slowly.)

One reason for the pessimism is the widespread fear of Japanese power. Japan's rate of economic growth is three times greater than that of the United States. With a population half the size, Japan is producing twice the number of scientists and engineers. Japan's savings rate is twice that of the United States. Savings are what produce investment, innovation, and growth. Japan sells to America three times what it buys from America. The imbalance in trade with Japan is an irritant and an embarrassment. So are purchases by Japanese firms of what have come to be called "trophy" properties in the United States, such as Mitsubishi's controlling interest in Rockefeller Center and Sony's acquisition of Columbia Pictures. Japanese ownership of corporate America is very small, less than 2 percent, smaller than Great Britain's, but these highly publicized transactions make Americans uneasy.

There are signs of growing tension in the relations between the United States and Japan. American protests against Japanese protectionist trading practices are becoming increasingly sharp. And the publication in Tokyo of a book entitled *The Japan That Can Say No* has made things worse. One of the book's authors is the respected former chairman of Sony, Akio Morita, the man who conceived the Walkman and did more than any other to persuade Americans to buy Japanese consumer electronics products. Morita is regarded as a statesman in Japanese-American relations, and it came as a shock to his many American friends to learn that his coauthor was Shintaro Ishihara, a virulent racist and a hostile national-ist. In his sections of the book, Ishihara argues that the white race has misunderstood and underestimated the ac-complishments of the Japanese and other nonwhite races, which he says "will be a barrier for [whites] in the coming civilization." Ishihara believes that technology is becom-ing the key to world power and that Japan is already in the lead. He makes the remarkable claim that the eco-nomic successes of Taiwan, Korea, and Singapore are partly due to lessons learned during the Japanese occupa-tion in World War II. In a passage of breathtaking under-statement, Ishihara writes, "We are aware that some neg-ative things happened under the Japanese administration, but it cannot be denied that many positive things were left behind." Some negative things, indeed—some of the worst war crimes in history.

Shintaro Ishihara is not an obscure polemicist; he is one of Japan's most widely known public figures, and in a poll taken in 1989, he was Japan's second most popular politi-cian. That Akio Morita would join him in a book of this kind may be a portent of serious trouble ahead between Japan and the United States. Both authors assert that the United States is in decline, and Morita says, "The time will never again come when America will regain its strength in industry. We are going to have a totally new configuration in the balance of power in the world."

Part of that new configuration of power is taking shape across the Atlantic, as the nations of the European Com-munity move toward a single trading partnership. These twelve countries together have an output of goods and services almost as large as that of the United States. The United States is far more productive than any one of them, but their combined production is soon likely to be larger. The twelve countries plan to eliminate all trading barriers among them by 1992, which will produce a huge single market of 320 million people, more populous than the United States, with a work force that, in many of their member countries, is better educated. Sometime in the 1990s they hope to have a single currency and a central banking system. If all these actions take place, the European Community will be a formidable competitor.

Another reason for discontent is the fact that other countries are earning billions selling products invented in America to Americans. Many countries have invaded the vast American consumer electronics market, selling video recorders, television sets, radios, copiers, computers, and other devices that were created in American laboratories years before. Japanese companies thrive in the automobile business, long an American preserve. In 1989, car production among the Big Three American automakers dropped 10 percent, to the lowest level since the recession of 1982, while the production of Japanese cars made in American factories owned by Japanese companies increased 36 percent. Americans know their country has a great talent for manufacturing and innovation, but they also know that foreigners today have a greater ability to transform American inventions into commercial products—which are then sold to Americans. "Made in the USA" has been replaced by "Invented in the USA—Made Somewhere Else."

The argument is now sadly familiar: The United States is behind the curve, unable to solve its problems at home and faltering abroad. Its lead has been shrinking for years, and it could be overtaken. There has been a dangerous decline in the productivity of American workers. There has been a stunning increase in the amount of debt Americans have run up at home and a corrosive increase in the amount the government has borrowed from abroad. At the beginning of the 1980s, the United States was the world's largest creditor; now it's the world's largest debtor. The payment of interest on that colossal debt will continue well into the next century and will make less money available for investment in the United States. Less investment in factories, schools, and transportation will mean a lower standard of living for many Americans.

It needn't turn out that way. The future can be reclaimed by an America that regains its will to succeed. But success can be achieved only by sacrifice and work, by a return to the spirit that made the United States such a colossus of energy and enterprise during World War II. Americans can accomplish miracles when they're aroused or frightened, as they were in 1941. But it is difficult to get them energized. It takes something like the attack on Pearl Harbor. Or Sputnik, the little satellite the Russians threw into space in 1957. In the absence of such threatening events, Americans have always tended to mind their own business, secure behind their oceans, comfortable in their own vast economy, confident that God and the future are on their side. That philosophy worked for a long time, but it is not a winning strategy in today's world. It is, in fact, a losing strategy.

Part of today's problem is that the United States faces no single, specific challenge. No Japanese fleet has bombarded our territory, wily Russians haven't ambushed us with a leap of technology, men from Mars haven't landed. The things that worry us today are the same collection of difficulties with which we have struggled for many years.

The problems have been covered in the newspapers, books have been written about them, television documentaries have been shown, speeches have been made, and laws have been passed. And nothing seems to change.

What the country needs is a peacetime Pearl Harbor to shake it up, to make Americans aware of the trouble they're in, to tap their energy and their willingness to work. The strength is there, but it is being sapped by a combination of weaknesses—a thousand wounds we find difficult to heal. We have weakened ourselves in the way we practice our politics, manage our businesses, teach our children, succor our poor, care for our elders, save our money, protect our environment, and run our government. Each of these weaknesses, by itself, would be manageable. But each cannot be seen by itself. They all constitute an interlocking web of lethal trouble for the future. When all are seen together, the totality of the peril is frightening.

Let us imagine an America in the next century that has not solved these problems. If the government's debt and the trade imbalance remain high, many more billions of dollars will flow to the foreigners who fund our debt and sell us their goods. These foreigners will take that money and spend it here. Foreign ownership of American companies and real estate will increase, and millions of American workers will report to employers from Asia or Western Europe.

If America continues to fall behind in the competition to develop new technology, the most profitable products of the twenty-first century will be designed elsewhere. Components of these new products will be manufactured in high-tech factories in other countries, then shipped to the United States for assembly by low-wage Americans working for companies owned by foreigners in factories called "transplants." The assembled products will be shipped to customers in other countries who can afford them.

If the American educational system is not reformed, more of the burden of teaching young people will fall on their employers. Education in those circumstances will be strictly vocational, limited to basic mathematics and language skills. It will produce a generation of American workers with only enough education to do the low-wage, low-level jobs at hand, incapable of creative careers in other fields, ignorant of their cultural heritage.

American agriculture will continue to be the world's most productive, but the family farm may finally disappear, replaced by giant agrobusinesses that will, in many cases, be owned by foreign companies.

If America can't rebuild its roads and bridges and adopt a new transportation technology to move goods and people, the efficiency of America even as a low-tech, low-wage production center will diminish. Some companies may be forced to build transportation systems for their own products.

If America's cities cannot be rescued from crime, drugs, and poverty, a separate urban underclass will become even more institutionalized, and cities will be far more dangerous than they are today. The hard culture of the inner cities, based on crime and alienation, will become permanent, with the attendant danger for all Americans.

In other words, a nightmare. An America humbled and humiliated. One wonders what political effect this situation may have, what demagogues it may create, what demands it may produce for the expropriation of property owned by foreigners, what calls for the repudiation of foreign debts. Or what battles there could be as groups of Americans fight over smaller slices of a smaller pie.

This is not just a fanciful worst-case scenario. Some of it is happening already. The United States is forfeiting the future. I see America falling behind, abusing its human resources and losing its position on the cutting edge of contemporary technology.

The best example of American superiority in high technology is the supercomputer. Supercomputers can process as many as 2.5 billion instructions a second. Supercomputers lead scientists into unexplored areas of basic research. Every country needs them. Ministries of defense use them to design weapons and departments of agriculture, to forecast crop yields. They simulate nuclear tests and weather patterns. For the big powers, they are essential to national security intelligence. In commerce, supercomputers make the competitive difference in the creation of new products. The companies that make supercomputers, service them, and design their software become deeply involved in the affairs of the companies and, sometimes, the governments that own them.

The United States is the world leader in supercomputers. Ahead of Japan, although Japan, which didn't make supercomputers until recently, now manufactures 28 percent of all the installed systems.

That is why the news was so disturbing when America lost one of its supercomputer manufacturers in 1989. The closing of Control Data Corporation's supercomputer division thinned the ranks of American companies that are engaged in this vital enterprise.

The company's decision to leave the race was an illustration of the way many American high-tech firms are forced to operate. Control Data, a pioneer in the field, had invested hundreds of millions in its troubled supercomputer division. It was losing money on supercomputers at the rate of $100 million a year, and how would Wall Street, with its appetite for short-range profits, react to those losses?

In Japan, reaction to an annual loss of $100 million in the development of supercomputers is quite different. Hitachi loses that much on supercomputers every year and calls it development. Hitachi is a huge company that had sales of $44 billion in 1988. If it needs more money, it can borrow from Japanese banks at low interest rates. American companies must pay high rates to borrow. The high cost of capital has a crippling effect on many small American high-tech firms.

Cray Research has been building the world's fastest machines for seventeen years; two-thirds of all the world's supercomputers have been built by Cray. Cray is a small company in Minneapolis that won its leadership position because of the genius of its founder, Seymour R. Cray; held it because of its investment in research and development; and prospered because of its ability to innovate. But Cray was in trouble in 1989, and its problems reflect the difficulties facing the American high-tech industry today. Its Japanese rivals are seizing more of the world's supercomputer market. Its American competitors are building machines called minisupercomputers that are cheaper and almost as powerful. Its earnings have suffered because its largest customer, the U.S. government, has cut spending on supercomputers.

It has also been largely shut out of what should be one of its most important markets, Japan. Traditionally, Cray has sold many of its machines to government laboratories, universities, and other public institutions, where the need for supercomputers is greatest. In Japan, that pattern is reversed. Cray has sold a number of supercomputers to Japanese firms, but only one to a public institution. To stimulate business, Japanese supercomputer makers offer discounts of up to 90 percent to the public sector in Japan.

The giants of Japan are on the march. Hitachi, Fujitsu, and NEC, the "Big Three," make billions selling many different kinds of products. They can well afford to lose money for years on their supercomputers. Fujitsu's sales in 1988 came to $16 billion; Cray's sales were $557 million. Fujitsu says its latest model will be twice as fast as Cray's latest supercomputer. Cray Research is an inspiring example of all that is good about American inventiveness and competitiveness, a pioneer on the frontier of technology. Its troubles are the troubles of America's future in electronics.

Electronics is a colossal industry that encompasses everything from simple radio sets to the most sophisticated computer chips, from videocassette recorders to telecommunications networks. The world market for electronics is huge: Sales in 1987 amounted to more than $460 billion. The United States is the biggest producer, but its market share suffered a calamitous decline from 1984 to 1987. In 1984, the United States sold 50 percent of all the world's electronics products; by 1987, that proportion had dropped a staggering eleven points to a market share of 39 percent. This drop took place while Japan and Western Europe were strengthening their positions. Neither has as large a market share as the United States, but the United States is declining and their share is growing. From 1984 to 1987, Japan's production of electronics increased by 75 percent, American production by 8 percent.

J. Richard Iverson, president of the American Electronics Association, said, "We're declining far more sharply than any of us really thought. It is obvious that American high technology is at risk. This shrinking of the United States' market share must be reversed."

The U.S. market share in the area of the smallest computers is shrinking. The world's desire for laptop and notebook-size computers has created a $2 billion-a-year worldwide business that is growing at the incredible rate of 40 percent a year. The United States was, until recently, the leader in the laptop trade. Zenith had 28 percent of the world market. But Zenith sold its computer subsidiary to a French company and now will concentrate on consumer electronics and high-definition television. That leaves the Compaq Computer Corporation the only major American manufacturer of laptop computers.

Ira Magaziner, an expert on electronics, told the *New York Times*, "I think Zenith will have a tough time. For example, the Matsushita Electric Corporation (a developer of high-definition television) spends as much on research and development as Zenith makes in total sales. In addition, Zenith is losing money on consumer electronics. You put that together with the fact that other companies in the consumer electronics business have their government's help and it looks like a pretty difficult situation for Zenith.''

America's lead in other parts of the worldwide consumer electronics market was lost years ago. Senator Ernest Hollings calculated that the U.S. share of the American phonograph market was 90 percent in 1970 and is 1 percent now, its share of the audiotape-recorder market has shrunk from 40 percent to 1 percent, and its share of the color television market has dropped from 90 percent to 10 percent. Those markets have been ceded to foreign manufacturers. And foreign competition is growing in many areas of more advanced electronic technology. Japanese engineers are now designing matchbox-size tape recorders with no moving parts, television sets that can be used as home computers, and telephones that can translate foreign languages.

The threat to America involves more than consumer electronics. It involves the critically important field of semiconductors, the little chips that are vital to every aspect of electronics. Here, the Japanese have doubled their market share in the past dozen years. Japanese companies now sell one-half the world's chips, the United States around 40 percent. Japan supplies 90 percent of the world's one-megabit chips, which can store more than a million pieces of information. These tiny chips are needed for everything from supercomputers to jet aircraft, and makers of the most sophisticated electronic equipment, including military contractors, must depend on Japan for supplies.

You can't run today's world without chips, but more and more, the United States, including its military, is dependent on Japan. A Defense Science Board report for the Department of Defense concluded some years ago that the future ability of the United States to fight a war was dependent on chips. Yet in 1989, a White House study group said American efforts to develop new superconducting materials were so fragmented that the United States is unlikely to survive a long-distance race in this field with Japan.

The irony of the situation, repeated over and over in modern technology, is that the basic inventions came from American laboratories. An example is the dynamic random access memory chip, called D-RAM, an essential component of computers. American scientists invented these chips and American companies manufactured them. But because of Japanese competition, which included the below-cost dumping of D-RAM Japanese chips on the American market, most American manufacturers dropped out of the competition. Japanese and Korean firms now control 90 to 95 percent of the world market.

This situation so worried some American companies that in mid-1989 they began an undertaking designed to change the way the United States handles its high-tech problems. A consortium of computer and computer-chip manufacturers, led by IBM and Hewlett-Packard, set up a joint private-sector venture called U.S. Memories, Inc., to manufacture the D-RAM chip and challenge Japan. No government money was to have been involved, and the cost was to have been $1 billion. Cooperation among American companies was preferable to allowing the Japanese to walk away with the market. But U.S. Memories had great difficulty attracting support in the chip industry, and early in 1990 it went out of business. There was, at that time, a glut of chips on the market, and prices were falling. Critics of industrial consortia were glad to see U.S.

Memories die because it would have represented a change in the old competitive, entrepreneurial way of doing business in America. An industry analyst at MIT took the opposite view. Charles Ferguson told the *New York Times*, "It's just another symptom of our inaction in the face of this really quite gruesome problem."

Joint ventures in high technology came late to the United States; Japan began using them decades ago. U.S. Memories was not the first American gamble on the future; in 1987, a consortium called Sematech was formed, funded by industry and government, for research and development in semiconductors. Its budget is $200 million a year, with $100 million coming from the Pentagon, a heavy user of computer chips. A government advisory committee recommended in 1989 that federal funding be substantially increased, but the Bush administration rejected the idea. The president's science adviser, D. Allan Bromley, told a Senate committee, "Even if such funding were available, it is unlikely that such an approach would work." Bromley was reflecting the White House belief that government assistance for endangered areas of American high technology is wrong because it would interfere with the workings of the free market. Bromley's testimony carried another message, however. It was an elegy to the loss of American leadership. Bromley said, "In many ways, what is happening to the semiconductor industry is a paradigm for what could happen to other U.S. industries, such as the computer and telecommunications industries, unless corrective actions are taken in the immediate future." No additional corrective actions were being taken by the White House, which means an uncertain future for the American semiconductor industry.

The example of the Sematech consortium has spurred

Europe's three leading producers of semiconductors to form a joint venture of their own. Philips, Siemens, and SGS-Thompson are investing $5 billion to develop a computer chip with more capacity than American or Japanese chips. This project was easier to assemble in Western Europe than it would have been in the United States because European antitrust laws are more easily relaxed when strategic technologies are involved.

It may be difficult for Americans to realize the importance of these tiny memory chips, these silicon wafers the size of a fingernail, these megabit devices employing a technology most of us cannot describe. Let us call on Shintaro Ishihara, who wrote, in *The Japan That Can Say No*, of the accuracy of intercontinental ballistic missiles. Ishihara predicted that for future generations of weapons deployed by the Soviet Union and the United States, only Japan will have the ability to produce chips smart enough to control missile guidance systems. He stated: "If Japanese semiconductors are not used, accuracy cannot be assured. It has come to the point that no matter how much they continue military expansion, if Japan stopped selling them chips, there would be nothing more they could do. If, for example, Japan sold chips to the Soviet Union and stopped selling them to the U.S., that would upset the entire military balance. . . . The more technology advances, the more the U.S. and the Soviet Union will become dependent upon the initiative of the Japanese people—this is getting crazy now, but the point is clear." In 1988, for the first time, Japan's capital spending on semiconductors exceeded that of the United States. Ishihara is not crazy. The point is clear.

．　．　．

It is also clear that West Germany and Japan are moving quickly on competitive technologies of a more basic kind. Imagine a train that would travel very fast, that would not pollute, that would use less energy than ordinary trains, that would run in any weather and would not wear out. Chicago to New York in a couple of hours, New York to Washington in forty-five frictionless minutes—downtown station to downtown station.

You can ride on such a train at 250 miles an hour today in Emsland, West Germany. Or on another, at 325 miles an hour, on the island of Kyushu in Japan. Both are experimental, magnetically levitated trains, Mag-Lev trains for short. They don't ride on tracks; they ride just above them, suspended in the air by electromagnets whose like poles repel each other and propel the train forward.

The technology was invented in the United States, but there is no American Mag-Lev train. The American government abandoned its effort to produce one in 1975 because of a budget cut. Today, with an air-travel crisis on its hands and with large American cities choking in automobile exhaust, the U.S. government may find that magnetically levitated trains are perhaps the only workable alternative. But the way things are going, the United States may be forced to solve its transportation problems by purchasing trains from Bonn or Tokyo. When the United States ignored its own invention, the Japanese and the West Germans went to work. Today, the West German system is under construction in Nevada, as part of a plan to connect southern California to Las Vegas. Plans have been made to use a Mag-Lev train to run from the airport in Orlando, Florida, to Disney World. If the United States doesn't move quickly on its own Mag-Lev technology, Mickey Mouse and Las Vegas high rollers will be traveling on trains developed in Emsland, West Germany.

In 1989, the Senate Committee on Public Works asked an advisory panel to look into the chances of developing an American Mag-Lev train. The panel reported that there is a chance for the United States to regain its lead, but the country will lose it forever if it doesn't act soon. It said the abandonment of this American invention, given the prospects of a world market for Mag-Lev trains, was an illustration of how the United States loses its technological edge. "That America walked away from this effort more than a decade ago," the panel reported, "is demonstrative of the commercial technology lapses our country is prone to stumble into, characterized most visibly by the forfeiting of billion-dollar markets in consumer electronics and dynamic random access memory semiconductors—two American inventions commercially exploited by Japan."

The development of an American Mag-Lev train would cost the U.S. government $750 million over six years, according to a plan set out by Senator Daniel Patrick Moynihan. Moynihan has persuaded Congress to appropriate a million dollars for feasibility studies, and the Department of Transportation is spending an equal amount, but these are tiny sums compared to the Japanese and West German investments. A coalition of American companies is asking for more federal support, but the request must make its way past the White House's bias against government intervention in the workings of the free market. Mag-Lev trains will earn huge sums for their developers in the next century, when the present rail and air systems become even more overloaded than they are

today in the United States, Japan, and Western Europe. But unless the United States moves more quickly than it is moving now, the jobs and the profits generated by this invented-in-America technology will go elsewhere.

The same thing is happening in the field of generating energy from the sun. Today, only two American oil companies are engaged in research on and development of solar energy. At one time or another during the past few decades, seven big U.S. energy companies were working on solar power, but most of them dropped out. That's one way to lose the future. When electricity generated by solar panels is as cheap as electricity produced by conventional generators, much of the world will plug into solar power. It will be an enormous international market. And it may happen in the 1990s.

Much solar energy is already being used in the developing world. Solar cells power irrigation pumps, generators for remote hospitals, and even radios and refrigerators where ordinary power grids don't exist. In Israel, thousands of houses have solar panels on their roofs. In the United States, solar panels provide power for space vehicles and are used in recreational vehicles, and a solar cell provides the light at the bottom of my garden steps. In 1988, sales of solar power were at record levels. It's a $200 million-a-year business, and it is growing at a stunning annual rate of 20 to 30 percent, which means billions of dollars in a few years.

The industry's goal is to make solar power inexpensive enough so that utilities will add solar power to their coal- and gas-fired generators. In 1989, solar power was three or four times as expensive as conventional electricity, but the price is coming down fast. Solar cells were developed for the American space program twenty-five years ago; since then, production costs have come down by as much as 90 percent. The goal is in sight.

So why are there only two American companies in the solar power business? Why did giants like Exxon, Shell, Motorola, and ARCO leave the field to others, after spending millions on research? The answer: There's no money in it, *as of now.*

These big corporations are not going broke, but today's emphasis on short-term profits makes it ever more difficult for a company to spend millions without knowing when a goal will be reached. A publicly held corporation may be the target of a takeover bid if a raider could argue that too much research was "wasting" the stockholders' money.

A kind of corporate fatigue took over in some companies. ARCO had been in the sun-power business for ten years when its chairman said he was "losing patience" with solar power. The company had invested $200 million and never shown a profit. ARCO Solar was sold in 1989 to Siemens, A.G., of West Germany, which said, "The addition of ARCO Solar's technology and attractive product range will put Siemens in a position to fully develop this fast-growing market." And to compete with Japan, which now dominates the world market in solar power cells.

The U.S. government hasn't been much help. In fact, Washington's role in promoting this energy of the future is in danger of vanishing. At the beginning of the 1980s, the U.S. government was spending $155 million a year. Currently, it spends about $35 million, and the Bush administration wanted to cut that amount even further.

This decision was made as the governments of West Germany and Japan were increasing the amount of money they spend on solar research. Japan's and West Germany's expenditures on power from the sun are now greater than the American government's effort to develop this promising technology.

The United States is in much the same position in the field of drawing power from atoms—fusion power. When I think of fusion power, I am reminded of headlines in the supermarket tabloids: SUGAR CUBE POWERS MILWAUKEE! Fusing atoms to produce almost limitless energy is nearly that amazing. If this technology can be made to work, more energy is produced than is put in; the fire is bigger than the fuel. Scientists think it may be possible, with commercial applications sometime in the next century. This technology could, indeed, transform the world, bringing cheap, safe power in abundance to every country. It could also make its producers rich beyond dreams.

Fusion power is an intoxicant for investors. Two scientists reported in 1989 that they had made a breakthrough in another process called "cold fusion." They said they had produced energy in a tabletop experiment that seemed astonishingly simple. There was great skepticism among scientists, but the University of Utah, where the results were disclosed, received calls from companies all over the world asking for information.

The process that is more likely to bring results is called "hot fusion." Atoms can be made to fuse at temperatures of millions of degrees centigrade, but that process requires tremendously expensive equipment. It means duplicating the power of the sun in a controlled experiment. The goal of fusion energy is so attractive that the American government has spent many billions of dollars supporting research. And until recently, it appeared that the first stage of experimentation would be completed in the United States, which for many years was the world leader in fusion research. The first stage is called "break-even," and it is achieved when the amount of energy produced equals the amount of energy expended. Break-even could take place at Princeton University in the 1990s.

But it could be achieved sooner than that, and by European, not American scientists. A joint European facility in Great Britain could produce break-even fusion by 1992. The National Research Council, which advises the U.S. government, reported in 1989 that the United States had lost its leadership position to Europeans. The European experimenters, according to the council, have twice the personnel, better equipment, and more help from private industry.

The National Research Council says that the loss of America's lead was caused by a massive reduction in federal support during the past decade. The United States now spends $350 million a year on fusion research, which sounds like a lot of money, but ten years ago, it was spending twice as much. In 1989, the Bush administration was talking about cutting the research budget even more. It is infuriating that after investing so much over the past thirty years, with such promising results, the United States is running out of money just when things are getting interesting.

In *The Graduate*, Dustin Hoffman was told that plastics was the key to wealth and happiness. If the movie were made today, the key might be high-definition television, HDTV. A high-definition television picture is at least twice as clear and sharp as what we see now on our screens, it reproduces sound as well as a compact disc, and it means billions of dollars in sales for the country that first gets it into production. The American Electronics Association predicts sales in America of $1.5 billion by the year 2000, growing to $6 billion by 2010. In the next century, worldwide revenues from HDTV and its associated products will be something like $50 billion a year.

Skeptics regard HDTV as a consumer product and they wonder if it will catch on. The first generation of receivers will cost $1,500, which is a heavy price to pay for a better picture. Will consumers pay? The failure of quadraphonic sound systems, originally hailed as a profit-making technology, is cited as a case in point. But there will be many profitable applications of HDTV technology aside from the consumer market, and many experts argue that the United States should make an effort to get into it first. HDTV is more than just better picture quality. Controlling the HDTV market will lead to a larger share of the international market for memory chips—semiconductors. New inventions, such as video memory and digital signal processing, are part of HDTV and will be part of the development of the next century's semiconductors. Who controls semiconductors will control the high ground of twenty-first-century technology: the market for personal computers, automated manufacturing equipment, and hundreds of other products. The technology of HDTV will affect not only consumer electronics, but supercomputers, telecommunications, medical equipment, and basic science.

The trouble is, it looks as though others have got there

first. It's the old story: We invented HDTV thirty years ago, but other countries are developing it. The Japanese government and a number of Japanese companies have invested hundreds of millions of dollars over a twenty-year period on HDTV research and development. Western Europe is now spending as much as $250 million a year on a joint HDTV project. The Europeans plan to introduce their HDTV system during the 1992 Olympic Games in Barcelona. Sony is already manufacturing HDTV receivers in Japan, and experimental broadcasts began in 1989. The Japanese have designed screens twenty-one feet high that show pictures of startling clarity. Several American companies are working on HDTV systems, but the foreign competition is ahead.

Congressman Edward J. Markey of Massachusetts, a proponent of a strong American effort to get into the race for HDTV leadership, says, "The Japanese and Europeans are in the eighth inning of a tightly contested game. And the United States is about to hop into the station wagon to try to find the ballpark."

The ticket of entry is expensive. Three dozen American electronics companies, including such well-financed giants as AT&T, IBM, Hewlett-Packard, and Apple Computer, said the price would be well over $1 billion in assistance from the federal government. To make the attempt to catch the competition would require low-interest loans and federal guarantees, along with a relaxation of antitrust laws. A consortium of companies would work together to manufacture HDTV products. The start-up costs are beyond the resources of any single firm. Furthermore, the companies argued, foreign competitors receive massive government support. The Japanese government has put about $350 million into HDTV. The American government in 1989 was spending about $30 million, and that was Defense Department money. The Pentagon worries, rightly, that American defense will suffer if the spin-off technology of HDTV is in foreign hands.

Now the United States is being asked to play catch-up, and we may have to become more like Japan if the project is to have any chance of success. Becoming more like Japan means bringing the government into partnership, through loans and subsidies, with a sector of American industry. That's the way Japan, Inc., helped build its giant companies, but the Bush White House is against it. Government-business partnership is called industrial policy, and free-market conservatives oppose it.

Government partnership with industry does raise questions: Should the government get to pick the winners and losers among American industries? If HDTV gets the U.S. government as a partner, won't other industries have a right to ask for similar help?

Other critics of the partnership scheme say that if HDTV has genuine prospects of success, it should be able to borrow enough money to develop the product. Roger Porter, the senior domestic policy adviser in the White House, said, ''As a general proposition, if there is a promising technology, we have the most fully-developed capital market in the world. If it's a good idea with a lot of promise, it will get funded through the venture capital market.'' That assertion raises a question: If HDTV is such a promising technology, why haven't the venture capitalists come running with money? Is HDTV too expensive? Is it too late in the game? Or is venture capital more interested in short-term profits than risky enterprises? Is venture capital less venturesome than we think?

The questions may be academic. The Bush administration has decided that support for HDTV is wrong because it would push the government into an industrial policy. It looks as though this $50 billion annual market is lost to the United States.

HDTV is one part of what the experts call the Information Age. This era will begin when everyone in the industrial countries—in every home, office, factory, laboratory, and classroom—will be linked through computers, smart phones, and television hookups to a world communications network. The technology is there, and in some countries, the networks are in place.

A bank in Toronto now processes all Visa and Master-Card transactions conducted by American cardholders in Europe. The bank is able to handle this profitable business because Bell Canada provides telecommunications service that isn't available in the United States. The United States is in seventh place in the international race to develop a modern communications network that will be able to serve the needs of tomorrow's consumers, businesses, and universities. American companies are hampered by regulations and delayed by the lack of a unified, comprehensive national telecommunications policy. The Bell companies, tied up in regulatory battles in the United States, are selling their expertise overseas.

Singapore and Hong Kong have established telephone switching centers that are far more sophisticated and far less costly to use than are systems that are available in the United States. Many multinational companies have leased private lines to Singapore, where calls and messages can be sent anywhere in the world at a fraction of the cost of calling directly from the United States. The implications are immense: The new technology makes the location of a telephone service irrelevant. Services that Americans associate with their own telephone companies, such as operator assistance and 800-number activities, can easily be provided from foreign locations.

There is much more at stake, however, than operator assistance or tallying the charges that credit-card holders ran up in Paris. The world will soon be doing most of its business through telecommunications networks, sending messages, letters, and computer data almost instantaneously along high-speed fiber-optic lines or satellite links. If the United States is not able to join this world network, billions of dollars and millions of jobs will go to the countries that can do the business.

The price of building an Information Age network in the United States will be huge and will require heavy government investment. Proponents of that support argue that the government helped pay for the interstate highway system and that the interstates of the future, moving information instead of goods, will be the telecommunications networks.

Japan, looking toward a world market, says it will invest $240 billion in the next twelve years on telecommunications equipment. The United States is still making policy decisions.

In all these technologies, from supercomputers to telecommunications, the driving force is research and development. R & D is the engine that pulls the train of modern technology. In a high-tech age, the amount of money spent by industry and government on R & D makes the difference in a country's standing in the world.

One of the clearest ways of measuring a country's ranking in R & D is to look at its patent applications. In 1960 the U.S. government approved 47,000 patents; fewer than 8,000 were granted to citizens of foreign countries. In 1987, the U.S. Patent Office approved 88,000 patents; 41,000 went to foreign applicants, of whom 17,000 were Japanese and 8,000 were West Germans. The firms with the most applications for American patents in 1987 were Canon, Hitachi, Toshiba, and General Electric. If this trend continues, most of the American patents that are granted in the years to come will go to foreign companies, a lot of them Japanese.

The amount of money a country spends on its R & D is important, but how it spends that money is equally important. The United States was a big spender on R & D in the 1980s and still spends three times as much as Japan. Private industry spent $69 billion in 1989. The federal government spends about $70 billion a year.

This amount sounds good, but there's a problem. The U.S. government spends about $20 billion a year on non-military R & D and $40 billion on defense R & D. Most of this imbalance took place during the Reagan years, when federal funding for defense R & D increased 80 percent. R & D funding declined in those years for education, energy, the environment, and NASA. The priorities of the Reagan administration were clear.

There are some civil benefits from military research, but most benefits are military. And in recent years, the emphasis has been on weaponry, not on high technology. Of the $40 billion that the Pentagon spends on R & D, only $3 billion goes to advanced technology.

At the end of the Reagan administration, however, the funding levels for military R & D were in a decline. Some warned that this decline could make the United States dependent on other countries for defense technology. Others saw it as an opportunity. Kostas Tsipis, a scholar at MIT, told the *New York Times*, "Maybe this is an opportunity, not a problem. Here you have these highly skilled people leaving the defense industry. At the same time, you have serious issues of competitiveness and the environment and other long-term research problems that our industries cannot afford to explore. The logical thing is to decrease federal funding in one area and increase it in the other."

Yet, with budgetary constraints as severe as they are, it is hard to see that transfer of talent taking place. And our competitors in the world, with smaller military obligations, will continue to spend less of their R & D money on defense and more on civilian R & D. When the amount spent is calculated as a percentage of the gross national product (GNP), the total value of a country's annual output of goods and services, Japan and West Germany invest a far higher share of their GNP in civilian R & D than does the United States. Other countries have an additional edge on the United States because they have higher savings rates, which provide more money for investment at lower rates of interest.

Michael Boskin, an economist, pointed out a few years ago that "other countries are spending a larger fraction than they used to on R & D. Even when we generate new technology, they embody it more rapidly than we do, since our investment rate is so much lower than any other advanced economy." Boskin is now the chairman of the President's Council of Economic Advisors, part of the team that is searching in the bare cupboard of the U.S. government for ways to stimulate R & D.

. . .

Even if money for the civilian side of American R & D is increased, there's another danger: There may not be enough American scientists and engineers to make use of it. The United States may run out of scientists in the next ten or fifteen years.

The statistics are frightening. Within the past decade, the number of American college students intending to major in science has decreased by almost 40 percent. In the 1960s, one in ten freshmen wanted a career in science; today, only one in twenty. Robert Bottoms, president of DePauw University, said that young people's attitudes about science have been changed by "the glamorization of the MBA" degree; by the availability of careers in the fields of "soft knowledge," such as marketing and public relations; and by a reduction in the number of science teachers in the high schools.

This decline in scientific studies represents a fundamental change in American education and a challenge to America's technological position in the world. From 1950 to 1970, the number of degrees awarded in the basic sciences increased fourfold. In those decades, carrying a slide rule or working in a laboratory was a mark of prestige on American campuses. And those young scientists created the American dominance of technology. Today, the image of the student scientist or engineer seems to be that of a nerd.

In 1985, the United States, with a population of about 240 million, awarded doctoral degrees in computer science to 240 Americans. The annual number of Ph.D.s awarded in that critical field has probably declined since then.

There has been a significant reduction in the interest of students in every scientific field: in all the biological sciences, all the physical sciences, and all areas of mathematics. Only in some liberal arts colleges has this devastating decline been resisted. As President Bottoms explained: "Because the graduate schools were full, we thought we were okay. But they were full of foreign nationals, most of them planning to return home. Within 10 years, there will virtually be no large home-grown batch of scientists available."

Half the doctorates in physics awarded by American universities in 1986 went to foreign students. In American graduate schools of engineering, half the assistant professors under age thirty-five are foreign. When they get a little older, many of these foreign professors and students will go back to their native countries. There is already a brain drain, especially among Asians. Korean executives told the *Wall Street Journal* that returning Korean students educated in America had cut five years off Korea's lag behind the United States in semiconductor technology.

For much of the past decade, there has been almost no new construction of engineering schools. Existing facilities are getting old. Foreign teachers fill many jobs, but there were from 1,300 to 1,800 faculty vacancies in 1989 in American science and engineering schools. And the federal government hasn't done its job: Over the past twenty years, federal investments in university research facilities dropped by 95 percent.

If the United States runs out of scientists and engineers by the turn of the century, who will replace them? Today's thirteen year olds? Hardly. The Department of Education in 1989 helped fund a study of the mathematics and science skills of thirteen year olds in several countries. The American children came in dead last, with lower scores than the Spanish, British, Irish, Canadian, and South Korean children. South Korean thirteen year olds were first. The comparison was devastating. South Korea is a developing country, nearly destroyed by war in the 1950s, with a population that was mainly poor farmers a few decades ago. The United States is an economic giant, but it is suffering from a softening of the brain. The Council on Competitiveness estimates that 60,000 mathematics and science teachers in our high schools are not fully qualified to do their jobs.

The secretary of education said the results indicated a "national tragedy." Lamar Alexander, president of the University of Tennessee noted: "The obvious conclusion is that unless we're careful, the Buck Rogers of the 1990s is going to be living in Seoul, South Korea, instead of Chattanooga or Chicago."

Buck Rogers was an interplanetary traveler in comic books. What about less ambitious travels in the real world? According to the National Assessment of Educational Progress, four out of five American seventeen year olds can't make sense out of a *bus timetable*.

The geographic illiteracy of all Americans is a melancholy cliché. A survey for the National Geographic Society reported that 24 million adult Americans could not find their own country on a world map; 44 million could not identify China or the Pacific Ocean. The younger they are, the less knowledge they have. Americans aged eighteen to twenty-four were compared in knowledge of geography with young people in several other countries, and the Americans came in last, behind Mexico and far behind Canada.

America's educational system is in deep crisis. Everyone knows it and has known it for a long time. Seven years ago, the National Commission on Excellence in Education stated, "If an unfriendly foreign power had attempted to impose on America the mediocre educational performance that exists today, we might well have viewed it as an act of war."

In 1989, the secretary of education, Lauro F. Cavazos, reported that since 1985, American high school students had flat or declining scores on college entrance examinations and an unchanged dropout rate. One out of every four high school students today does not finish school—close to one million young people. Another fourth—another million—who are graduated are functionally illiterate when they get their diplomas. Half the eighteen year olds in this country today have failed to master basic language, mathematics, and analytical skills. A million dropouts here, a million functional illiterates there, *every year.*

The cost is colossal and so are the implications for the work force that is going to have to compete with European and Japanese workers. (Ninety-five percent of young Japanese graduate from senior high school.) The Center for Educational Research at Stanford University claims that the cost to the United States of one year's high school dropouts is nearly $3 billion in lost earnings and lower tax revenues over the lifetime of that single class. And it happens every year.

Functional illiterates not only cost money, they can't find even low-skill jobs in our changing work force. The proportion of unskilled jobs will decline from 9 percent of the work force today to 4 percent in the year 2000. The country's need for skilled workers will increase from 24 percent today to 41 percent in 2000. In 2000, nearly one-third of the available jobs will require a college degree.

The failure of the high schools has damaged the ability of the universities to do their jobs. Vartan Gregorian, the president of Brown University, said,

> In the midst of the explosion of information, knowledge and complex challenges facing us, the American university cannot afford the luxury of transforming its first two years of instruction to meet the woeful inadequacies of our public school system. We cannot afford to relegate 50% of the university's time and resources to remedial work. . . . The universities in two years cannot do justice to twelve years of neglect in learning. We are our high schools' keepers. The nation must take preventive measures to reform, strengthen and in some cases rescue our high school system.

A college education has become prohibitively expensive. The cost of tuition at public universities in the 1980s went up six times faster than family income; for private universities, the increase was nine times greater. The squeeze was on the students, their families, and their bankers. Federal grants to students dropped, and loans increased. Today, half the student aid in the United States is borrowed money that must be repaid. That may be why fewer young Americans are now going to college, just when the country needs them.

The paradox is that the United States spends more on each student than does any other industrialized nation. Education in America, from kindergarten through graduate school, now costs $353 billion a year. The federal government's share of that expense is $30 billion. Yet the products of this system are so lacking in skills that American business must spend about $25 billion a year to educate new workers.

There's a saying among teachers: If you think education is expensive, try ignorance. Education is tremendously expensive in the United States, but what we are getting for our money is ignorance.

Something else that robs America of its competitiveness is poverty. The poor are not productive, and the price of poverty to the society is high.

The plight of black Americans is especially serious, in part, because there are 30 million of them, and so many are poor. More than one out of every eight Americans is black, and about one-third live in poverty. In 1989, we learned that progress made by blacks, the social and economic gains that began in the 1940s, that so gripped the country in the 1950s and 1960s, stopped around 1970. The National Research Council said there had been no significant progress for the past twenty years, that a "great gulf" still separates the races. Its study showed that the plight of blacks goes beyond racial prejudice, that "if all discrimination were abolished today, the life prospects facing many poor blacks would still constitute major challenges for public policy." Discrimination hasn't been abolished, and the council doesn't think it will be any time soon; it noted that the participation of blacks "in a color blind society is unlikely in any foreseeable future." The council found that blacks face higher levels of discrimination in housing than do other minorities: The residential separation of whites and blacks is twice as high as the separation of whites and Hispanics or whites and Asian Americans. The council's judgment is that things aren't going to get any better; that a third of all black people will continue to live in poverty; and that in certain areas, such as wages paid to black men, things could get worse.

The high level of poverty in the United States places the country in a bad position as it heads into a period of intensified competition with Western Europe and Japan. Japan has no minority problem; the country is 99.4 percent ethnic Japanese. Japan has virtually no poverty problem. The United States, however, must carry into its competitive wars 9 million black Americans who are officially below the poverty line. That's more people than live in Sweden. American businessmen ask for a level playing field when they compete with foreign companies, which is a fair demand, but too many of their players have to sit on the bench.

Nearly 12 million American children are officially described as living in poverty, one out of every five. That's the figure for all children: It is much worse for minorities. Nearly half the black children in this country live in poverty, as do 40 percent of Hispanic children. The U.S. Bureau of the Census indicated that the percentage has grown in recent years. The Children's Defense Fund stated that the rate of poverty for children increased by almost one-third from 1979 to 1987.

That so many American children live in poverty is a disgrace to the world's leading economic power. Other industrial countries treat their children far better than we do. In a comparison of seven countries published by the Urban Institute, the United States had the highest percentage of children living below the poverty line: more than three times higher than that of Sweden, more than double the percentage in West Germany. The study showed that the American poverty rate is high because American government programs for the poor cover fewer people and provide fewer benefits than do programs in other industrial countries, even though family incomes are higher in the United States than in most of the other countries in the study.

America, in fact, treats its children badly in general. According to Peter G. Peterson and Neil Howe, in their book *On Borrowed Time*, the federal government currently allocates *eleven times* more benefit dollars per capita to Americans over age sixty-five than to children under age eighteen. If you're under eighteen, you can't vote. If you're over sixty-five, you can—and you do. The elderly are probably the most potent political group in the country. So, for every dollar Washington spends on children, it spends eleven dollars on old folks. Poverty is declining among the aged. Since 1970, the poverty rate for the elderly has been cut in half, while the poverty rate for families with children has doubled.

Children are our future. The quality of their education and the state of their health will determine how competitive and how strong America will be in the next century. Today, we are cheating our children, especially the minority children who will be perhaps one-third of the work force in the difficult and competitive times of the 1990s. It is a moral failure of the first magnitude and a catastrophic strategic mistake that saps our strength and endangers our national security.

■ ■ ■

The United States is squandering its lead and losing its technological edge. The effects of drift are manifold. What is under way, unless drastic action is taken, will result in the most serious threat to American economic power since the Great Depression of the 1930s.

On August 21, 1989, a Tokyo newspaper reported that Japan had become the world's richest nation. Japan's most respected economic newspaper, the *Nihon Keizai Shimbun,* said it based its assessment on 1987 statistics from Japan's Economic Planning Agency and the Federal Reserve Board in Washington. The 1987 figures were the latest available.

The *Nihon Keizai Shimbun* said the United States in 1987 had assets—real estate, factories, securities, inventories, bank deposits—worth $36.2 trillion. According to the Economic Planning Agency in Tokyo, Japan's assets that year amounted to $43.7 trillion.

All these assets, of course, are only on paper and have to be taken with a drop of soy sauce. Some of the Japanese wealth is based on overvalued Tokyo real estate, some of it on the appreciation of the yen against the dollar. In financial assets, the Japanese could be ahead. But not in real assets. The United States still produces far more goods and services than does Japan, it has twice as many people, and its land area is twenty-five times larger. In terms of tangible assets, there is no way that Japan could be ahead.

Yet the thought occurs that there may be a deeper truth here: that Japan is *winning,* that the Japanese have found a way to outproduce the United States, and that the Europeans are finding it now. In the early years of the twenty-first century, the degeneration of America's competitive position may become irreversible.

A kinder, gentler America is an agreeable concept, but it is not a remedy for the ills that plague the United States today. What is urgently needed is a tougher, smarter America. And there's not much time left in which to achieve it.

PART TWO

America, 1970-90: How Did a Country So Rich Get So Poor?

After midnight on December 7, 1972, a burst of brilliant light lit up the Florida sky, followed by a rising column of flame that could be seen from North Carolina to Cuba. The astronauts of Apollo XVII were on their way to the moon, riding a giant Saturn V rocket. It was the first night launching of a moon mission. The heavens, from horizon to horizon, became an enormous reddish-gray canopy, the world's biggest tent, lit by the blast of the rocket. Those of us who had covered the manned space program and had watched many launches had never seen anything as spectacular.

We would not see it again. An exhilarating chapter in the history of the planet was coming to its close. Apollo XVII was the end of NASA's manned exploration of the moon. The program had lasted only four years, an amazingly brief span of time, from the first flight around the moon in 1968 to the final mission on the lunar surface in 1972. NASA wanted to make additional flights, but the public got bored and the money ran out. Humankind's greatest adventure had been brought to an early end by competing national priorities and the costs of the war in Vietnam. Public support for the exploration of the moon had begun to diminish even before Neil Armstrong stepped on the lunar surface in 1969. NASA's budgets had been declining since 1966. In Vietnam, although the last

American combat troops were leaving, the war was still costly. Space exploration was wonderful, but the country had other things on its mind that December night.

The year 1972 was one of the last of the good years in America. The country had been scarred by Vietnam and the turbulence of the 1960s, but most people still held the beliefs that had been bred into them since the end of World War II. For almost three decades, Americans had learned that each generation would be richer than the one before it. It was an American birthright. To say that America was number one was accurate, not arrogant, in the early 1970s. No other country came close to the stupendous fecundity and wealth of the United States. In those years, America was not only the richest country in the world; it was producing more goods and services than the *combined* output of Britain, France, West Germany, and Japan.

Despite this prosperity, there were signs that things were going wrong. Unemployment was rising because of a world industrial slowdown. In 1970, the United States had incurred its first foreign trade deficit since 1888. Americans were getting poorer. Household income had begun to decline, hourly wages were going down relative to the cost of living, personal debt had begun to rise, the number of families living below the poverty line was increasing, and the gap that separates the rich from the poor was growing wider.

Small cracks began to appear in the mighty American economic machine. Investment in new equipment began to slow down, which resulted in a decline in the rate at which the productivity of workers increased. New equipment makes workers more productive. During the good years of the 1960s, industry invested heavily in new equipment, and productivity rose. In the 1970s, the rate at which productivity increased was cut in half. The fault was not a lack of technology; it was less investment in new plants and machines. Productivity doesn't make big headlines, but it is a vital component of growth and prosperity.

The other reason for America's economic slide made big headlines. War in the Middle East caused the first of the oil shocks of the 1970s. Israel had been attacked by Egypt and Syria in the Yom Kippur War of 1973, and President Nixon airlifted $2 billion worth of American arms to Israel. In retaliation, Arab oil-producing countries imposed a ban on petroleum exports to the United States. In 1973 the United States was using cheap petroleum at a reckless pace, and one-third of its oil came from foreign producers. The country wasn't prepared for a shortage, and the Arab ban created chaos. Some motorists waited for gas in lines that were one mile long, an unprecedented inconvenience in a country filled with stations selling gas at thirty-five cents a gallon. It was another lesson in the limits of American power.

The embargo, however, was only an annoyance compared to what happened next. OPEC, the Organization of Petroleum Exporting Countries, raised its prices, striking at one of the main sources of American prosperity. The boom years of the 1950s and 1960s were made possible by crude oil at five dollars a barrel. Petroleum goes into everything from gas tanks to phonograph records. All the industrial countries—the United States, Japan, and those in Europe—counted on cheap oil. But some members of OPEC, including America's friend the shah of Iran, wanted price increases. Giant increases. And they got them. During the Yom Kippur War, OPEC members raised their prices by 70 percent. Later in the year they raised them again by 128 percent. Nothing that happened in the 1970s was as economically harmful as was this devastating increase in the cost of energy. When the decade began, the United States was paying $3 billion a year for imported oil; by 1980, the price was $62 billion. The result was a dangerous decline in growth and a deadly increase in inflation.

The country was struggling with other problems in the early 1970s. The defeat in Vietnam threw its shadow over everything. Demonstrators in the streets and on the campuses insisted the war had been a colossal moral blunder. Americans recoiled in horror when four Kent State students at a rally protesting the war were shot and killed by national guardsmen. There were ugly scenes caused by antiwar militants. Some American troops returning from the war were spit upon when they reached West Coast ports; others were afraid to wear their uniforms when they got home. Americans who had supported the war were embittered by the government's failure to use enough force to win it, a debatable argument, given the fact that the United States had spent billions fighting the war at a human cost of 58,000 dead and 153,000 wounded. Some said that whether or not the United States should have gone to war, the conflict was simply unwinnable. There were many who blamed the press for reporting only the bad side of Vietnam. Military officers complained that their hands had been tied by the politicians. Some politicians believed they had been misled by overoptimistic generals. Everyone blamed everyone else, everyone took a position, and there seemed to be no center of opinion, only angry arguments made by people who had made up their minds.

It all came to a sorrowful end in 1975, when the American Embassy in Saigon was evacuated. Few will forget the sight of helicopters taking off from Saigon with South Vietnamese desperately hanging on to the skids, some falling to their deaths. Most Americans believed that getting out of Vietnam was the right thing to do; at the same time, they knew it was wrong to abandon the South Vietnamese. The psychological damage left a large scar. The Korean War twenty years earlier had given the United States its first experience with an unwinnable conflict. Vietnam was an unpleasant lesson in the limitations of American power. Our easy, almost casual, sense of omnipotence, our certainty that America was both powerful and decent, were shattered by Vietnam.

It wasn't only Vietnam that sapped the American spirit in those years. Richard Nixon and Spiro Agnew were reelected in November 1972. Eleven months later, Agnew became the second vice president ever to resign. The first was John Calhoun, who resigned in 1832 because he differed with President Andrew Jackson on tariff policy. Agnew's problem wasn't tariffs; it was taxes. He pleaded no contest to charges of income tax evasion, was put on probation, and was fined $10,000. Other criminal charges, of bribery, extortion, and conspiracy, were dismissed. Gerald Ford, the Republican leader in the House of Representatives, was named to replace him.

People were asking what the country had come to, with the resignation of the vice president and suggestions that the president himself might be impeached. The virus of Watergate began to coil through the American mind. The country talked of nothing else and seemed to watch nothing else. On all the networks, John Dean, former counsel to the president, told the Senate Watergate Committee that Nixon himself, his staff, his campaign workers, and the Department of Justice had participated in the Watergate cover-up. The Senate Watergate hearings went on month after month, with daily disclosures of wrongdoing, as millions watched.

Televised impeachment hearings by the House Judiciary Committee began in the spring of 1974, and by midsummer, the great wheel of the U.S. Constitution began to turn. The committee recommended three articles of impeachment. Some of its members wept in the committee room after voting to approve the first article; so did some in the press seats. In August, the House of Representatives, without debate, accepted the committee's recommendations by a vote of 412 to 3. But by then, Richard Nixon had resigned and gone home to California. Gerald Ford was president.

The country had watched all this unfold in the greatest detail. Some of it, especially Nixon's resignation speeches and his departure from the White House, produced wrenching drama. The nation was shocked, dismayed, and divided. Some said Nixon had been driven from office by a conspiracy of the press. Some said he got what he deserved. Conservatives fought with liberals, Republicans with Democrats, wives with husbands, parents with children, friends with friends. Watergate had a corrosive effect on America's morale. It was something new in the American experience. Before Watergate, criminal conspiracies, like the Teapot Dome scandal in the Harding administration, involved government officials using power to get money. But in Watergate, officials, including the president himself, used money to hold on to power. Cash, some of it from a White House safe, was used to finance the cover-up. As the Watergate conspirators grew more and more desperate, they used every tool at their command to protect themselves and the president, but the heart of it all was the use of money to retain political power.

The United States was built around a central idea: that the people would rule without a monarch. Yet, in modern America, the president embodies some of the attributes of a king. The presidency is almost a sacred office in our secular society. A president is never personally addressed by his name, only by his title, Mr. President. Special music is played only for the president: "Hail to the Chief" and "Ruffles and Flourishes" are reserved for the chief executive, the commander in chief. And, in what is the ultimate royal prerogative of the twentieth century, a president is the only person in the United States who can appear, whenever he chooses, on all the television networks simultaneously.

In Britain, the queen reigns but does not rule; she is head of state. The prime minister, elected by Parliament, is head of government. A head of state is a useful institution. When a prime minister stumbles or when a government falls, the state, the central embodiment of the nation, is untouched. When an American president, head of state *and* head of government, is forced to resign, the country is shaken to its foundations.

When Nixon was forced out, confidence in the institution of the presidency was splintered. Agnew's *nolo conten-*

dere plea on tax evasion and Nixon's tacit admission that he had violated his oath were twin disasters separated by just ten tormented months.

What effect did this barrage of deceit have on the American spirit? Did it lessen the willingness of Americans to work, study, sacrifice, save, and invest? National morale is the product of many things. The spirit of a country is made up of its songs, jokes, expectations, and disappointments. Economic activity involves more than markets, inflation, tax rates, or investment. People behave as they do because of the culture in which they live, and the culture is shaped by many factors, some of them intangible. Japan's culture is more responsible for its relentless productivity than are the laws of supply and demand. Confucius is more important to the Japanese than is Adam Smith. Material things are not the only motivation for economic decisions. A researcher at the University of Michigan found a correlation between the public's fear of nuclear war and a low national savings rate. That makes sense. Why put money in the bank if you're likely to be blown up?

Let us, therefore, examine the mood of America's workers after Agnew and Nixon had walked the plank. The country's two senior elected officials had turned out to be, well, crooks. Washington couldn't be trusted. The CIA had been acting like a rogue elephant. *The Pentagon Papers* proved that the government hadn't told the truth about the war. The loss of Vietnam was still a painful memory. Many Americans came to realize that the real suffering of the war had been imposed on the middle class and the poor, and they felt that had been unfair. Poor kids had fought and many had died. Rich kids had gone to college or to Canada. It was shown that few members of

Congress had sons or daughters who had served in Vietnam. A fault line began to separate young Americans. The Democratic party, traditional defender of working people, was perceived as being controlled by feminists, gays, blacks, and ultraliberals. Political assassinations, the shame of the nation, hadn't stopped; George Wallace was shot in 1972. The economy was in trouble. Against that background, did anyone expect American workers to march off to their jobs every morning, heads high, singing patriotic songs? Or to stop at the bank on payday to put money in savings accounts?

Nixon's disgrace led to another disappointment: Ford granted him a pardon. What did *that* mean? Was it the last act in a White House conspiracy? Hadn't Nixon given Ford his job as vice president at a time when Nixon knew he might be impeached? Ford's explanation seemed reasonable: After what the United States had gone through in the Agnew and Nixon resignations, all the anger and humiliation, the last thing it needed was a lengthy, protracted criminal proceeding against a former president. There had been enough media circuses. Still, there was suspicion that Nixon had traded the office of the presidency for a presidential pardon. At around that time, trust in government was falling fast. Cynicism increased. Ten years before, according to the University of Michigan's Institute for Social Research, 76 percent of Americans had high levels of trust in the government in Washington. By 1974, that percentage had been cut in half. The trust Americans had in their national government would fall even further as the difficult decade wore on.

Ford was sensible, calm, and decent, in vivid contrast to Nixon. The White House arranged for cameras to record him making his own breakfast, and there was a sigh of relief across the country as Americans watched him toast his muffins. The tensions of the Nixon presidency, the arrogance of the Nixon White House, were replaced by the plain vanilla administration of a friendly, middle-aged, middle-class man from the Middle West. Ford's great ambition in life was not to be president, but Speaker of the House, where he had served for twenty-five years. Jefferson said the presidency was a "splendid misery," and there were times when Gerald Ford seemed to agree. He is a much happier man today than when he was in the White House.

Ford was an accidental president who was prone to little accidents. He had a tendency to hit his head on doors or to fall down on the ski slopes (it happened once when the cameras had been assembled to show the public how well he skied). In fact, Ford was fit and well coordinated, a former college athlete, but he couldn't shake his reputation for being physically awkward. On a visit to Austria, he slipped and fell on an airplane gangway as the cameras rolled. The television newscasts made much of it, and everyone laughed in a good-natured way about clumsy old Jerry. Old Jerry, however, wasn't clumsy. Later that day in Salzburg, I watched a slow-motion videotape replay of his fall and was astounded by his quickness: When his feet went out from under him, he swung his arm away from his wife so as not to drag her down, kicked his feet backward, threw his body forward, and made a four-point landing as gracefully as a cat, all in a couple of seconds. Jerry Ford was more than he appeared to be. His problem politically was that he didn't appear to be up to the job. Many Nixon haters believed that the crook had been replaced by the klutz. A klutz was not what the country needed just then.

The economic danger signals of the early 1970s had turned into crisis-level concerns by the time of Nixon's resignation. Some of these problems were beyond the ability of the United States to control. But a question needs to be asked: Would the economic news have been so bad in Nixon's second term if Nixon had not been immersed in his own defense and, at the end, preoccupied with his own survival? In 1972, when Nixon ran against the hapless George McGovern, he was reelected in a landslide comparable to Franklin Delano Roosevelt's 1936 triumph over Alf Landon. Nixon had widespread popular support before the scandals engulfed his administration. If there had been no Watergate, might this consummate politician have devised ways of helping the country help itself? He had not flinched in 1971 when he ordered wage and price controls, suspended the conversion of the dollar into gold, and asked Congress for a surcharge on imported products. He took these draconian measures to combat inflation and high interest rates, and less than a year later, interest rates had dropped and the rate of inflation had been cut in half. It was a shock and a reversal of his conservatism, but it worked. In 1972, he turned away from a lifetime of anticommunism and made new friends in China and Russia. But in 1973 and 1974 Nixon was so crippled by Watergate, his popularity had fallen so low, that he would have had neither public nor congressional support for bold economic initiatives, even if he'd made them. So, for two crucial years, as its economy weakened, just when it needed strong leadership, the United States was led by a dispirited, beleaguered, and—in the end—powerless president. Richard Nixon committed many sins; the greatest was leaving the country without leadership at a time when it needed a leader desperately.

■ ■ ■

The OPEC oil shocks caused a world recession. Economic growth slowed in the United States. Unemployment was high. The year 1974 was the peak year for strikes since the end of World War II. The purchasing power of the dollar was dropping. Inflation reached double digits: consumer prices rose 11 percent in 1974.

The national savings rate started a long decline in these years. Savings are the key to growth: savings provide money for investment, investment buys new machines, new machines allow workers to produce more, producing more creates additional wealth, the economy prospers, and living standards go up. One of the tragedies of the 1970s and 1980s was the low American rate of savings, while the Japanese rate remained so high. The savings rate in 1973 was a normal, healthy 9.4 percent of disposable personal income. It dropped every year after that until it reached its low point in 1987, when it was a dismal 3.2 percent. As much as any other factor, the low American savings rate contributed to the country's economic woes. The difference was made up by foreign investments in America, which is not bad in itself, except that it is another part of the mortgage on America's future.

The rise in prices was the most obvious problem during the Ford years, and President Ford began a campaign to fight it called "WIN," which stood for Whip Inflation Now. It was a lackluster effort. Buttons were printed with the letters WIN, and the president wore one. His campaign against inflation helped a little, but inflation remained a problem for the rest of the decade. People were grumbling about a sick economy as they celebrated the bicentennial. There were complaints about the quality of

American workmanship. Detroit cars made on Mondays and Fridays were said to be inferior to cars made in mid-week because the workers were hung over on Mondays and bored on Fridays. It was a telling comment in a dispirited time.

What was less noticeable but perhaps even more important was a change in the way American industries viewed their profits and their management. During the 1970s, a theory was developed that a good manager could manage anything, that the principles of management did not necessarily stem from knowledge of what was taking place on the shop floor. A new breed of all-purpose managers appeared, and in many companies they replaced the old-line managers who had a deeper understanding of what the company was actually making. In some firms, what the company was making became less important than the performance of its stock. Quarterly reports on profits had to look good to keep the value of a company's stock high. In many companies more effort went into generating profits than into long-term planning. A lower priority for hands-on management, research and development, and strategic investment was another reason why productivity slowed and the standard of living of workers declined.

The pride that Americans had in their country was being worn down, as people compared their past accomplishments with their present status and worried about their prospects for the future. This sense of disenchantment was most apparent in the condition of the American automobile industry.

The 1970s brought the foreign car to the United States, and all those little Hondas and Toyotas brought with them a great change in American attitudes and a blow to American self-esteem. The United States had been the world's unchallenged leader in the production of automobiles. In 1965, twenty years after Japan's defeat in World War II, Americans had owned half the world's automobiles, nearly all of them made in America. That year, the United States imported only 26,000 vehicles from Japan. In 1976, it imported well over 1 million. From 1975 to 1980, Americans bought 16 million foreign cars and trucks, half of them Japanese. Detroit autoworkers were enraged by the success of the imports. Signs went up in the parking lots of plants that read, "If you're driving a Japanese car, don't park it here—park it in Tokyo!"

One reason for the success of the imports was that they got more miles per gallon than did American cars. Worry about mileage was a new experience. Getting good mileage had never, in peacetime, been a top priority for American drivers. Gas was always cheaper in the United States than almost anywhere else, and it still is. In 1974, a gallon of gas cost fifty-three cents in the United States. The same amount cost $1.36 in Japan and $1.27 in West Germany. Fuel efficiency was important in Germany and Japan, countries that had to import oil, so these countries made automobiles that got many more miles per gallon than did American cars. When OPEC drove up the price of oil (and hence the price of gas), Detroit was stuck with gas guzzlers, while West Germany and Japan were ready with fleets of small econoboxes that got great mileage. The foreign cars were cheap to run, the doors went *ka-chunk*, and nobody worried whether they had been built on Mondays or Fridays.

The automobile is an American icon. Cars and trucks transformed this country. Getting one's first car is a rite of passage for teenagers. Many Americans drive cars until they're eighty or even ninety years old. Most of us can't live without them. I wonder what the rise in high-quality cars that are designed and produced in other countries has done to the American psyche, to our sense of self-confidence. Has it led to a national inferiority complex?

The mass production of well-made, affordable automobiles and trucks was invented in America. A new car is a symbol of status. One of my uncles never kept his Buick more than a year before he traded it in for one that was essentially identical. His car was always new, smelled new, ran new. Detroit obliged him with planned obsolescence, a few cosmetic details added each year to make the cars look slightly different, but few improvements in the machinery. Americans were urged to buy big automobiles because Detroit had a bias against small cars, since they produce lower profits than big family sedans. And Detroit has been slow in improving technology. A recent study by MIT pointed out that the last home-grown innovation in American cars was the automatic transmission, introduced in the 1940s. Other technologies, including antilock brakes, four-wheel drive for passenger cars, and turbochargers appeared in cars made by foreign companies before they were utilized by American manufacturers.

There was great frustration in the 1970s about the success of German and Japanese automakers. People asked, Who won the war, anyway? Many were embarrassed when they bought cars made by foreigners, but they bought them by the millions, nevertheless. The great American icon had been shattered. We were no longer the unquestioned world leader in automobiles.

And suddenly it seemed as though everything else came from Sony, Hitachi, or Mitsubishi. Most radio and television sets were being made outside the United States, and home video recorders came from Japan. Those smart foreigners had outfoxed us again. An American company, Ampex, had perfected videotape recording and was making large, expensive recorders for professional use. But Ampex didn't get into the consumer side of the business. Japanese firms did and reaped billions in profits. We had Hondas in our garages and Sonys in our living rooms. It must have been around then that a large number of Americans began to believe that Japan was number one economically. Skepticism about American institutions, a healthy tradition, began to shift to cynicism. During the gasoline shortages in 1976, many believed that the oil companies were holding back supplies to drive up the price. Camera crews from the networks were dispatched in airplanes to get pictures of tankers hiding at sea, loaded with oil. No tanker fleets were found, but the rumors persisted.

Gerald Ford served as president for two years and five months. He lost the 1976 presidential election to Jimmy Carter, who squeaked in with 50.1 percent of the vote. An electorate bruised by Watergate, suspicious of the Nixon pardon, frightened by unemployment, weakened by inflation, distrustful of Washington, and pushed around by OPEC wanted a change. Ford was the first president since Herbert Hoover to campaign for election and lose.

In his two-year run for the presidency, Jimmy Carter had capitalized on the country's reaction to Nixon's excesses. Carter declared his candidacy four months after Nixon resigned, and he ran, in part, on a promise that he would never lie to the American people. His opponent was Gerald R. Ford, but Carter really ran against Nixon, speaking in coded phrases about truth and honesty. It was understandable politics: Who would not have used Watergate against the Republicans? But the effect of Carter's campaign was to keep the memory of Nixon's crimes before the public. When he moved into the White House, the first movie he ordered to be shown was *All the President's Men,* the story of Watergate.

Part of Carter's success was that he ran against Washington, the first Democrat in memory to do so. American attitudes toward the role of the federal government were changing in the 1970s. The New Deal and its successor Democratic party programs had been in place for forty years. Four Democratic presidents and three Republicans—Eisenhower, Nixon, and Ford—had hardly touched the edifice of liberalism that Roosevelt had constructed. Nixon had expanded federal programs for housing, education, and aid to the poor. But by the 1970s, the fundamental goals of the New Deal had been largely achieved. People began to worry about the size of social programs and the taxes needed to pay for them. In California's famous Proposition 13 balloting, the voters rebelled against high property taxes. That rebellion was repeated in many other states. Carter talked passionately about bringing the federal government under control, about cutting waste, about making the government more efficient, and about balancing the budget. That was just what the public wanted to hear.

It was time for something new, and Carter provided a fresh kind of political theater. Cartoonists made fun of his country ways. One drawing showed an outhouse on the White House lawn, as Carter's mother, wearing a sunbonnet, smoked a corncob pipe. Carter worked hard on his image as a simple countryman. His favorite game was softball; he taught Sunday school in a Baptist church near Plains, Georgia; and he carried his own garment bag (someone picked it up one morning and discovered it was empty). In many ways, he waged a brilliant campaign that touched on all the troubles and anxieties of the people, a campaign that persuaded them to vote for a candidate most of them had never heard of a year or so before. The American people were yearning for change and chose a stranger to lead them. Carter got their hopes up. They picked him and they got change, but the frustrations and disappointments were to continue and grow worse.

From the year in which Jimmy Carter won to the year in which he lost the presidency, inflation more than doubled. In 1980 consumer prices rose more than 13 percent, the prime lending rate was over 15 percent, and there was a seven-month recession. In the Carter years the cost of a gallon of gas almost doubled because OPEC raised its prices again. The United States began to import less oil, but OPEC charged more for it. There were, again, shortages and long lines at gas stations.

Yet, despite the gloomy economic situation, Americans continued to spend. Consumption of imports soared. The money spent on foreign cars and trucks almost doubled, and spending on other imported goods more than doubled. People may have been pressed for cash, but spending on foreign products kept rising.

How could Americans spend more when their wages were stagnating and their living standards were being eaten away by inflation? They did three things: They continued to save less money, they went ever more deeply into debt, and more and more women got jobs to make ends meet. From 1972 to 1979, 11 million women got jobs and went to work. That caused a profound change in American life: Day-care centers became a necessary service for millions of young families; more and more young children were left to fend for themselves after school; more meals were eaten in restaurants than at home. The old Norman Rockwell image of the family around the dinner table had been replaced by Mom, Pop, and the kids at the fast-food franchise eatery.

Why did Americans want to spend more? One reason may have been an increase in cynicism. There was an attitude of what the hell, who cares? Jimmy Carter's pollster, Patrick Caddell, told the president that the public's mood was so sour, so cynical, and so disenchanted that people would simply ignore a presidential warning about future oil shortages. Caddell had found that the public was convinced the government *and* the oil companies were either incompetent or dishonest or both. Caddell's surveys convinced him that the American people were rapidly losing faith in themselves and their institutions. Governance was not easy with that feeling in the air.

By the middle of 1979, Jimmy Carter was in serious political trouble. Senator Edward Kennedy was talking about challenging the president in the 1980 primaries. The president responded with uncharacteristically coarse language, pledging that if Kennedy tried, he'd "whip his ass." When Jimmy Carter talked that way, he was getting tense. Carter's approval rating in the Gallup poll dropped 17 points in three months. An ABC/Harris poll in June showed that only 25 percent of its sample approved of Carter's performance. Richard Nixon's lowest rating, when he resigned, had been at about that level.

In July, the president shut himself up at Camp David for an unprecedented period of soul-searching, while

Americans wondered what he was up to. Some of the most influential figures in politics, business, and labor and even a few journalists were invited to visit the president at his mountain retreat and discuss the state of his presidency and the mood of the country. Governors, members of Congress, religious leaders, and economists were among his guests. He said later that all were helpful except the economists.

Carter emerged to deliver a remarkable speech, called "Energy and National Goals." It was more about goals than about energy. Carter began by saying:

> The true problems of our nation are much deeper . . . than gasoline lines or energy shortages, deeper even than inflation or recession. . . . It is a crisis of confidence. . . . We've always had a faith that the days of our children would be better than our own. Our people are losing that faith, not only in government itself but in their ability as citizens to serve as the ultimate rulers and shapers of our democracy. . . . For the first time in the history of our country a majority of our people believe that the next 5 years will be worse than the past 5 years. . . . The productivity of American workers is actually dropping and the willingness of Americans to save for the future has fallen below that of all other people in the Western world. . . . What you see too often in Washington and elsewhere around the country is a system of government that seems incapable of action. You see a Congress twisted and pulled in every direction by hundreds of well-financed and powerful special interests.

Carter's cabinet had been invited to watch the speech on television in the White House. Joseph Califano, who was secretary of health, education and welfare, recalls that he was amazed by the speech. Califano asked himself, "How could we run against Washington and government when the President was both?"

Carter continued, "We are at a turning point in our history." He said solving the energy crisis "can also help us to conquer the crisis of the spirit in our country" and he asked his audience to save energy by taking no unnecessary trips, to use carpools or public transportation, to park cars one extra day a week, to obey the speed limit, and to lower thermostats to save fuel. He concluded, "Whenever you have a chance, say something good about our country."

It was instantly called "the malaise speech," even though Carter never used the word. In the short run, it helped politically; Carter's standing in the polls went up ten points. But in the long run, Kennedy used it against him and so did Ronald Reagan. Both said, with false piety, that *they* could find no "malaise" in the American spirit.

It was an astonishing performance from a politician who was planning to run for reelection. Carter seemed to be echoing Walt Kelly's assertion that "We have met the enemy and he is us." It was a jeremiad that no president had given before. Americans weren't saving enough, they weren't confident enough, they consumed too much, too many of them tended to worship self-indulgence, and they were disrespectful of their institutions, all of which, Carter warned, posed "a fundamental threat to American democracy."

Yet it was an accurate description of the United States at the end of the 1970s. There *was* a crisis of the American spirit. The government in Washington couldn't control inflation or interest rates. Living standards were going to hell. The country was filling up with foreign products and foreign cars. The political system was clogged and unresponsive. And there was enormous anger that the Arabs in OPEC were gouging America. OPEC is made up of thirteen countries, only seven of which are Arab, but most Americans (and apparently all editorial cartoonists) think the cartel consists exclusively of evil-looking Arab sheikhs wearing long robes. People asked what was America coming to, if it could be pushed around by a bunch of Arabs?

That feeling of rage and impotence was lodged in the American mind like a time bomb when Carter gave his malaise speech in July 1979. The bomb would go off four months later, when the American Embassy in Tehran was seized and Americans were taken hostage.

Since before the end of the Vietnam War, Iran has caused the United States more trouble and given American presidents more headaches than any other country. The strength of the shah was misjudged by Richard Nixon. The strength of his opponents was misjudged by Jimmy Carter. The Iran-Contra scandals damaged Ronald Reagan's reputation. In the early months of the Bush administration, word came of the murder of an American hostage in Lebanon by a terrorist group supported by Iran. The White House worried about another outburst of public anger, but by then, Americans had learned to keep their emotions in check when confronted by terrorist outrages. The Iranian roller coaster had turned into a long, downward straightaway. But the roller coaster had provided a wild ride.

Nixon had seen the shah as the policeman of the Persian Gulf and a pro-American guardian of Russia's southern flank. He allowed the shah to buy new armaments before they were delivered to the American armed forces. Even the OPEC oil-price disasters, which the shah helped bring about, didn't diminish Nixon's affection for him.

The shah was actually a megalomaniac who bullied the Iranian people and used secret police to keep them under control. He was both arrogant and insecure. He wore elevator shoes, but he believed he had a divine mission to modernize his country. He dreamed of replicating the power and influence of Cyrus the Great, who ruled the Persian Empire in the sixth century B.C. In 1976, the shah's rubber-stamp parliament approved a new Iranian calendar based on the coronation of Cyrus. The shah was the first Iranian monarch to be educated in Europe, which produced, according to Robert Graham, "a cultural schizophrenia." In *Iran: The Illusion of Power*, Graham wrote that the shah had "an admiration and fascination with Western culture, technology and institutions and yet a strong, almost chauvinistic attachment to the values and traditions of Iran."

The shah was impressive and incomparably regal. On his visits to New York, he would sit in his suite at the Waldorf Towers and tell reporters, "I'm buying some jet fighters for my air force," as though he'd been purchasing thoroughbred mares for his horse farm.

In those years, the opposition to the shah's regime was growing. But the Nixon White House thought the shah was in an impregnable position. So did the Carter administration, until it was too late. American diplomacy and American intelligence missed the boat in Iran. But nobody knew that during the glory days of the shah's wealth and power.

As many as 35,000 Americans—salesmen, technicians,

and advisers—were in every part of Iran. The American Embassy staff swelled to more than a thousand U.S. diplomats and military officers. New York filled up with new Iranian billionaires who entertained royally in new Iranian restaurants and made many friends. The shah wanted Iran to be a developed country, European style, which may have been the goal of his new billionaires, but was not an idea embraced by most of his subjects. One Iranian said, "He wants us to be Europeans, but we know we'd always be second-class Europeans. We want to be Iranians."

The Carter administration, despite the growing opposition to the shah, continued the alliance. The shah gave a New Year's Eve party at his home in Tehran in 1977, attended by the president of the United States, the king of Jordan, their foreign ministers, and a crowd of superrich Iranians. A few of us in the press were there, goggle-eyed at the lavish hospitality. At midnight, on the shah's high-fidelity system, Guy Lombardo's orchestra played "For Auld Lang Syne."

Carter called Iran "an island of stability," which was diplomatic politesse. Iran was falling apart. The shah had about a year left on the throne. His secular ways and his forced modernization had for years offended conservative Moslem extremists, followers of the Ayatollah Ruhollah Khomeini. As the conservatives' strength grew, the shah tried martial law and a military government, but nothing worked, and he was forced to leave in January 1979. Two weeks later, Khomeini returned from exile to a frenzied reception by millions of Iranians. The giant American gamble on Iran had been lost.

The shah wandered from country to country, finally to Mexico. The mobs in Tehran had turned against the

United States, and there were wild demonstrations. Washington was urging all Americans remaining in Iran to leave. The American Embassy staff was reduced to about seventy-five people. American intelligence listening posts near Iran's border were under siege. For several days, twenty U.S. Air Force employees were held prisoner by Iranian militants. All the signs read "danger."

Word then came to the White House that the shah was gravely ill and needed urgent medical attention, which could be given only in the United States. David Rockefeller and Henry Kissinger beseeched the president to let the shah come. Carter's instincts were against it because Iran might retaliate; the American Embassy in Tehran had warned that the Iranian reaction might be severe. But Carter gave in. He permitted the shah and his empress to fly to New York.

Thirteen days later, 3,000 conservative Moslem militants swarmed into the American Embassy and took a number of hostages, including 62 Americans. Their demand was that the United States return the shah and his money to Iran and *apologize to the world* for "crimes against the Iranian people."

The hostage crisis produced an avalanche of bitterness and outrage in America. The malaise of which Carter had spoken was a feeling, a mood, but sixty-two American hostages were grim, cold facts, hard evidence of the limitations on American power and the helplessness of the United States. The affront was intolerable.

The time bomb in the American mind went off.

For the next fourteen months, the fate of the Americans imprisoned in the embassy was the absolute center of American attention. Nothing was more important than the hostages. People hung yellow ribbons on trees. The national Christmas tree in Washington was not lighted. Churches held prayer vigils. The hostage crisis was on television all the time, in the newspapers every day, in the magazines every week. The world's press flowed into Tehran to record the parades of Iranians that passed endlessly in front of the American Embassy and the vast crowds that assembled to hear the Ayatollah Khomeini, the high priest of the Shia branch of Islam. There is much grace, serenity, and beauty in the Moslem world and the Moslem religion. But to Americans, the Tehran demonstrators looked *insane*—alien and fanatic. That added to the torment.

Some Iranians were astonished at the amount of news coverage. Sadegh Ghotbsadeh, the Iranian foreign minister who would later be executed by his fellow revolutionaries, told me that his government had been surprised when the militants took the hostages. But, he said, the new government decided to take advantage of it. The shah had constructed a sophisticated television network in Iran. Ghotbsadeh said that the Khomeini revolutionaries put the demonstrations at the embassy on television to show Iranians that the revolution had succeeded. The television pictures, he complained, were not designed to make Americans angry but to make Iranians proud, to consolidate the revolution. The pictures, however, made Americans very angry, and they were on every day.

The Tehran transmitters, operated by cooperative revolutionaries, poured out pictures to the American networks. Anchormen on CBS and ABC began opening and closing their newscasts with reminders of the hostage story, as in, "Good evening on Day 3 [or 30, or 256, or 425] of the Iranian hostage crisis." We did not do this on the "NBC Nightly News" because we felt it would needlessly institutionalize the crisis, which looked as though it might last a long time. ABC and CBS persisted, thereby reminding their audiences of the hostages even on days when there was no hostage story. Producers like to end newscasts with lighthearted or funny stories. One evening, CBS showed one that made Dan Rather roar with laughter—until he remembered his duty to look serious and say good night on "day" whatever it was of the hostage crisis. It was embarrassing.

There is nothing that should, or could, have been done to limit news coverage of these events. The reporting of the hostage story was fair, if sometimes overblown. There was, in fact, some self-censorship. A few of us in the American press knew that six American diplomats had taken refuge in the Canadian Embassy when the American Embassy was seized, but that story was not reported until the diplomats were out of Iran. Nevertheless, the magnitude of the coverage of the hostage crisis, the constant repetition, the special sections in the papers, and the special programs on television added greatly to the anger and despair of the American public. The United States was a decent and civilized country. Now it was being called "The Great Satan," and there was nothing that could be done. The hostage crisis made Americans feel frustrated and weak.

Americans didn't feel any better when the Soviet Union moved into Afghanistan at the end of the year. That invasion led to another disappointment: The United States pulled out of the 1980 Olympic Games in Moscow. Farmers were unhappy when the administration stopped the sale of American wheat to the Soviet Union. The Senate's ratification of the SALT II treaty on nuclear weapons became politically impossible, and Carter asked

the Senate not to consider ratification. Many people remembered that when the president had signed the treaty
in Vienna earlier that same year, Carter and Leonid
Brezhnev ended the ceremony in an embrace. Among
those who remembered was Ronald Reagan, a candidate
for the Republican presidential nomination.

The hostages were seized on November 4, 1979. Two
days later, the White House started planning for a rescue
operation. It took five months to create the plan, assemble
the equipment, and train the rescue force. The operation,
named "Eagle Claw," was to have five interlocking
phases: (1) American commandos were to be flown in
transports to a place in the Iranian desert designated as
Desert One, where they would rendezvous with helicopters; (2) the helicopters would fly the commandos to a
hiding place in the mountains designated Desert Two; (3)
a fleet of trucks purchased by the CIA would ferry the
rescue force into Tehran, where the commandos would
rescue the hostages; (4) the helicopters would fly into the
city, pick up the commandos and the hostages, and fly
them to an abandoned airstrip near Tehran; and (5) transport planes at the airstrip would fly everyone to safety, and
the helicopters would be abandoned, all secret equipment
aboard them destroyed. If any one of these links failed, the
whole operation would collapse.

There seems to have been a suspension of reality at that
time in the White House and the Pentagon. Senior officials apparently believed that the rescue mission would
not put the hostages in mortal danger, that the hostages'
captors, who had been described as crazed fanatics, would
not put them to death if attacked. Secretary of State Cyrus
Vance was the only high-level official to object. The president thought, and so instructed the Pentagon, that the

mission could be accomplished without many casualties and, unbelievably, with *no American casualties*. Carter's diary records what he told the Defense Department: "We want it to be quick, incisive, surgical, no loss of American lives . . . minimal suffering of the Iranian people . . . sure of success."

This tooth-fairy optimism doesn't represent military thinking. It is political thinking that wants a guarantee of no American casualties; it is presidential pie-in-the-sky thinking that wants a commando operation, full of blood and danger, to be carried out without risk, sure of success. And it is only civilians who believe that there are such things as "surgical" strikes.

The hostage rescue mission, as it turned out, didn't endanger the hostages because it got nowhere near them. It was a humiliating debacle that made the United States a laughingstock. And it was another blow to American morale.

Everything went wrong, right at the beginning. The mission was aborted at Desert One because not enough helicopters got there. One helicopter, in the swirling dust of that mad desert midnight, crashed into a transport plane loaded with fuel and ammunition. Eight men died; three were badly burned. The rest of the force escaped on overloaded transports. The helicopters, with secret equipment intact and secret papers undestroyed, were left behind for the Iranians. The government in Tehran gleefully published pictures of the burned-out helicopter that were shown all over the world.

What happened at Desert One was a perfect illustration of the clogged arteries of the American military establishment. The basic problem was that every branch of the armed forces was involved, each with its own system of communication and command. The army supplied Rangers and the commandos of Delta Force. The navy supplied ships. The air force provided the transport planes. The marines contributed the helicopters. The CIA supplied the trucks and the drivers. Everybody wanted a piece of the action, and under the American military system, which encourages interservice rivalry, everybody had to be involved. There was no single unit in the armed forces that had all the required equipment under a single command.

None of the services could communicate with the others because the radios of the various services were tuned to different frequencies. The helicopters couldn't talk to the ground at Desert One. The Rangers on the ground couldn't talk to the air force. Delta Force couldn't talk to the Rangers (but was in communication with the White House). There were, in all, five different military units in the rescue force. None had trained with the others, and many of the men had not met their fellow warriors when they got to Desert One. There had been no general rehearsal.

When the decision was made to abort the mission, there was great confusion. Arthur T. Hadley, in his book *The Straw Giant*, described the scene at Desert One:

> Imagine the hostile, alien darkness; the blowing sand from the six helicopters still on the ground, all with their engines going to guarantee a restart; the heat and sweat and noise; the piles of heavy equipment like camouflage nets; and the fear and the haste and the disappointment. At this confused moment, who is giving orders to whom? What is the command picture, as they call it in the Pentagon? There were four commanders there on the desert

floor, wearing no identification marks, equipped with radios that did not work together, and having no agreed-upon plan of operation. Each did not even have a designated place to stand.

President Carter blamed it all on fate. In his diary, he wrote, "The cancellation of our mission was caused by a strange series of mishaps—almost completely unpredictable. The operation itself was well-planned. The men were well-trained. We had every possibility of success."

The president was misinformed. It was not a strange series of unpredictable mishaps. It was a failure of the United States to train and equip a commando force capable of rescuing hostages. Other countries have such forces, including Britain, West Germany, Italy, and Israel. Perhaps none of these countries' forces could have brought sixty-two hostages out of the crowded center of Tehran. But they would not have been as vulnerable to misfortune as were the Americans.

The casualties of Eagle Claw were many. The dead and wounded men. The loss to the administration of Secretary of State Vance, who handed in his resignation before the mission began. The dispersion of the hostages, which made any further rescue attempt impossible. But the biggest casualties were the prestige of the United States and the morale of the American people. The eagle had no claws.

Since the end of the Vietnam War, there has been a change in the way the United States uses its military power. Presidents today want assurances of safety and success, political insurance policies that are militarily impossible. Senior officers want broad popular support for military actions. Nobody wants another Vietnam. The hostage rescue mission was one example among several. For the invasion of tiny Grenada, the Pentagon assembled an armada. When the White House ordered an air strike against Muammar al-Qaddafi's headquarters in Libya, it insisted that the planes make only one pass over the target, to reduce the danger of American casualties, a restriction that limited the mission's success. The battleship *Iowa* was used to bombard Lebanon instead of aircraft because strong air defenses on shore would have put the lives of American pilots at risk. The result was an inaccurate and politically damaging bombardment. The Bush administration's invasion of Panama in 1989 was an exception; a large body of U.S. troops was engaged in heavy fighting. But, in general, the post-Vietnam military operations of the United States have been carried out in such a way as to avoid hazard—to the uniformed forces that carry out the missions and to the politicians who send them. Presidents now demand happy endings, but in Jimmy Carter's case, he didn't get one.

Seven months after the disaster at Desert One, Carter lost the presidential election to Ronald Reagan. The American hostages were still in captivity. The failure to rescue them or negotiate their release was a factor in Carter's defeat, but there were other reasons. As he campaigned, prices were going up at an annual rate of 12 percent. Average weekly earnings, relative to the cost of living, had declined. There were more than 7 million unemployed, and the unemployment rate in some rustbelt cities was 15 or 20 percent. The prime lending rate was 15 percent. That much bad news was too much to overcome. When Ronald Reagan asked voters if they believed they were better off than they had been four years before, the answer was clearly no. Carter became the *second* incumbent president since Herbert Hoover to campaign for reelection and lose. Two in a row.

The United States had undergone a succession of failed, flawed, or tragic presidencies since the early 1960s. President Kennedy was murdered. President Johnson was forced to pull out of the 1968 election because of Vietnam. President Nixon had to resign in disgrace. President Ford couldn't win in 1976, nor could President Carter in 1980. A revolving door at the White House was something new for Americans, most of whom had grown up under presidents who had lasted longer. Franklin D. Roosevelt had been in the White House for twelve years, Harry S. Truman for seven, and Dwight D. Eisenhower for eight.

It is also arguable that the presidents of the 1960s and 1970s were not of the highest quality. John F. Kennedy was an inspiring leader who died before his full potential could be displayed, and we will never know what kind of president he would have been. In recent years the public has learned of the flaws in his personal life, hidden at the time by his staff and a few in the press. Lyndon B. Johnson was a titanic force in domestic affairs, but his Vietnam policy was a disaster. Richard M. Nixon accomplished much, but demeaned the office more than any other president. Gerald R. Ford was an amiable man who helped clean up after Watergate, but otherwise accomplished little. And Jimmy Carter, the outsider, wasn't able to come to grips with Washington and the sea of troubles that engulfed his administration.

All these men did good and important things, but none is going to make a list of great presidents. That fact should come as no surprise. The United States has had only a few presidents who were great. When things were going well, during most of our history, the United States prospered under mediocre presidents. But the extraordinary challenges in recent years—the Vietnam War, the rising competition from overseas, the economic troubles of the 1970s—demanded extraordinary leadership. We needed a great president but couldn't find one.

Presidents make a difference. The White House is infinitely more of a bully pulpit today than it was when Theodore Roosevelt was president. The White House produces more news, if its publicity releases and press briefings can be called news, than any other institution in the United States. Hardly an evening passes when the president is not on the network news; hardly a morning goes by when the president is not covered exhaustively in the newspapers. Neither of the other two branches of the federal government can match the executive branch in its command of the national agenda.

The White House attracts the best minds in and out of government. Proximity to the president acts like a narcotic on the most intelligent people in academe, government, and business. The staff has grown enormously in size and influence over the past few decades and is the dominant force in the federal bureaucracy. What has been created is a machine for leadership that is more powerful than any other in our society—or in any other country, for that matter.

On a few occasions in recent years, presidents have used the machine to great advantage. Carter took the president of Egypt and the prime minister of Israel to his country retreat and virtually locked them up until they emerged with the Camp David Accords. Nixon, using Henry Kissinger as a secret emissary, began the opening to China and created a period of détente with the Soviet Union. Give Nixon his due: In one swift, decisive move in 1971, he separated the dollar from gold and, for good or ill, began the breakdown of an international monetary system established in 1944. Not all the intractable problems of the world can be solved by a president, but the power of the office to shape events is still awesome. Moreover, the Constitution places the chief executive at the center of the action; Congress is both constitutionally and politically incapable of executive leadership.

A paradox of our time, however, is that most recent presidents have used the wonderful machinery of the White House badly. Reagan, assisted by a top-notch political staff, used it well in his first term but ineptly in his second. Reagan's flawed second term followed the pattern of the previous four presidents. Johnson tried and failed to use the platform of the presidency to persuade the public to go the full distance in Vietnam. Nixon at first created an imperial White House, with trumpeters in ludicrous operetta uniforms, and when the laughing subsided, he sank beneath the weight of Watergate. Ford and Carter often seemed bewildered by the levers of power.

If these men had been medieval kings, they might have been called Lyndon the Devious, Richard the Crook, Gerald the Unready, and James the Incapable. For the American people, they represented seventeen years of hopes raised and hopes dashed.

The people then turned to Ronald the Enchanter.

. . .

In 1976, the voters picked a former governor from the South with no Washington experience. In 1980, they chose a former governor from the West with no Washington experience. That's all the two had in common. Carter struggled with the minutiae of government. Reagan didn't care about details. On some occasions, instead of giving him briefing papers, his aides would prepare a videotape for him to watch. Carter on television seemed like a country preacher. Reagan at his best was an American Demosthenes.

Reagan had a clear vision of what he wanted to accomplish, simple, understandable, clearly stated, and politically appealing. He wanted to cut taxes, to decrease government spending on domestic programs, to increase spending on defense, and to balance the budget. He would lessen the size and scope of the government, make America strong again, and balance the country's books. The heart of Reaganomics was the theory that lower tax rates would stimulate the economy and make workers and businesses so prosperous that their tax payments would increase and balance the budget. Reagan had said in the campaign, "Balancing the budget is like protecting your virtue: all you have to do is learn to say no." There was a breathless innocence in Reagan's hope that the budget could be balanced by 1984. It was an astonishing pledge, given his plans for taxing and spending, and he never made good on it. His final economic message promised a balanced budget by 1993, and few believed that prediction either.

Democrats and Republicans regarded Reagan's plan as fantasy. George Bush had called Reagan's scheme "voodoo economics," and Howard Baker, Republican leader in the Senate, said Reaganomics was a "riverboat gamble." There was doubt that Reagan could reach any of his goals. But the president surprised everyone by reaching some of them almost immediately.

In the summer of 1981, the Congress passed two seminal pieces of legislation that set the agenda for the Reagan era. One cut taxes by $747 billion over five years, the largest single tax cut in history. The other cut federal spending, mainly on programs for the poor. The enactment of legislation of this magnitude so quickly was an unexpected display of presidential power. How he did it helps to explain Reagan's influence with Democrats in Congress.

The Republicans had won control of the Senate in the 1980 election and had gained thirty-three seats in the House of Representatives. Members of Congress believed a strong conservative tide was running, symbolized by the election of the new president. That belief made it possible to persuade conservative Southern Democrats, called Boll Weevils, that it would be in their political interest to vote for what the White House wanted. Reagan didn't persuade these Democrats through charm or salesmanship; the critical factor was that the election results and the public opinion polls convinced them America was turning to the right.

The cuts in taxes and domestic spending resulted in the first redistribution of income in favor of the affluent since the 1920s and a reduction of the federal government's obligation to the poor. Lower taxes made Republican voters happier with their party; the Democrats were weakened because there was less money for programs that helped the old Democratic constituencies: low-income

workers and the poor. Programs for the politically powerful middle class escaped. The Republican plan in 1981
was to break up the old Democratic alliance of middle-
and low-income voters and replace it with a Republican
alliance of middle- and upper-income voters. It didn't
work, and one reason was the steep recession that started
that year. The hard times drove many voters back to the
Democrats, and the elections of 1982 increased the Democrats' strength in Congress. The chance for a significant
political realignment died in the recession.

Next came the increases in spending for defense, $1.5
trillion in Reagan's first six years. Many Americans have
a misconception about the big defense buildup; they
think Reagan started it. The buildup actually began years
before he got to the White House. Defense spending
started to increase under Gerald Ford. When evidence
appeared of a serious Soviet buildup, Jimmy Carter
speeded it up. If Carter had been reelected, his plans for
the Pentagon called for annual increases larger than the
budgets that were actually approved under Reagan. In
the public's mind, however, Reagan got the credit, or the
blame, because he was such an enthusiastic hawk.

The combination of much more money for defense and
much less tax revenue was the chief reason for the mount-
ing deficits. Yet Reagan wasn't as big a tax cutter as the
public believed. He didn't like to talk about it, but the
government actually took in more money during his time
in office than it did in the previous eight years. The great
tax slash of 1981 was followed by the large tax increase of
1982. Reagan allowed taxes to be raised every year from
1982 until 1988. He may have hated it, but he did it. Why
didn't you know about it? Because he didn't tell you.
While he was in office, he signed eighteen tax bills, thir-

teen of which increased the government's revenues. A little bit here and a little bit there, in what was called "revenue enhancement." But the tax hikes weren't big enough to offset the huge deficits.

Another reason for the soaring deficits, beyond Reagan's control, was the inflation he inherited. Benefits under some entitlement programs, including social security, increased as the rate of inflation increased, and that added hundreds of billions to the debt. In turn, more debt pushed up the cost of interest, adding more billions.

Reagan had inherited a national debt that was heading for a trillion dollars. That amount was too much, he said. In his first speech to Congress, he said if you had a trillion dollars in thousand dollar bills, it would make a pile 60 miles high. Little did he know. When he left office, the national debt was about $2.6 trillion, which would make a pile of thousand dollar bills more than 150 miles high. Under Reagan, there was more of a buildup of the national debt than under all previous presidents. The combination of big tax cuts, big increases in defense spending, and a hair-curling recession did the job.

The recession was the worst since the Great Depression of the 1930s. At one point, almost 12 million people were out of work. Reagan's popularity rating dropped sharply, and in the 1982 elections, the Republicans lost twenty-six seats in the House. The GOP paid heavily for the recession, but there was a political bonus when it ended. Inflation had been beaten. With Reagan's approval, Paul Volcker and the Federal Reserve Board had leached inflation out of the economy by driving up interest rates. Higher interest rates drove down business activity. The resulting recession killed inflation. It was probably the most important economic development of the Reagan era because it set the stage for years of economic growth. It was not without cost, however. The government has to spend more during a recession, on things like unemployment programs. It takes in less during a recession because slower business activity produces lower tax revenues. The recession drove the country ever more deeply into debt. The deficits became a permanent, unwelcome guest at the table. America had swapped crippling inflation for crippling deficits.

By Christmas 1982, the recession was over. The great Ronald Reagan extravaganza was about to begin. Reagan's supporters, despite evidence to the contrary, claimed that a Reagan revolution was taking place, a shift toward conservatism, comparable to the massive political realignment brought about by Roosevelt and the New Deal. Some meaningful changes did take place. There was an increase in the number of people who called themselves Republicans, especially among the young. Confidence in government went up. There was a feeling that America was more respected in the world and stronger militarily. That feeling led to increased support for negotiations on nuclear arms. During the Reagan years, Daniel Yankelovich, the public opinion analyst, discovered a significant shift in the willingness of Americans to strike a deal with Moscow. Americans were wary of negotiations during the Ford and Carter presidencies because they believed the United States was less strong than the Soviet Union. When Reagan persuaded them that America had achieved at least nuclear parity, if not superiority, a sizable number of people told Yankelovich's pollsters they were ready to negotiate. That was an uplifting bit of news; when the American people felt stronger, they became more peaceable.

. ■ .

Perhaps the most important political result of the Reagan presidency was a shift in the frame of reference. The terms of debate changed. The old arguments about enlarging the role of government were replaced by discussions of where to cut it. The presence of the deficits stifled talk of new programs. Some believe that Reagan accepted the deficits, even planned for them, because he knew they would reduce the scope of the federal government. Whether that belief is true, the Reagan deficits accomplished what politics couldn't: Washington's role in the life of the nation has been significantly reduced, and that was one of Reagan's primary goals.

Yet what Reagan accomplished was far short of a revolution. Barry Goldwater complained toward the end of Reagan's second term that there had been no revolution at all. Reagan's presidency produced no fundamental change in public attitudes toward social issues, it did not reduce government spending, and it did not get the government off the backs of the people. Government spending in Reagan's fifth year was substantially higher than in his first, when calculated as a percentage of the GNP.

Reagan, in fact, was a timid conservative whose actions were rarely as strong as his words. He said he wanted a Constitutional amendment to ban abortion and spoke often about prayer in the classroom, but he never fought hard for those objectives. They are controversial, hot-button issues that create hazards for politicians. He was against gun control and the Equal Rights Amendment, but for all his popularity and skill in communication, the public's support for gun control and the ERA didn't change during his presidency. He wanted to do away with domestic programs enacted by Democrats, but most of them remain in place, operating on lower budgets, still there, waiting to grow. The middle-class entitlement programs, such as social security and veterans' benefits, were largely untouched. The United States was a middle-class welfare state when Reagan came in, and it was a middle-class welfare state when he went out.

Not a revolution, but something important happened to the United States during his eight years.

I call it the Reagan Enchantment.

When Reagan became president, most Americans were weary of one-term presidents and were looking desperately for someone of heroic size who could do something about the country's problems. Of those polled by Gallup, 78 percent said they were not satisfied with the way things were going in the United States. People were fed up. The country had lost in Vietnam, been humiliated in Iran, and hurt by inflation. People were worried about unemployment and they were being killed by high interest rates. Jimmy Carter had lectured them on the crisis of the American spirit. Reagan would have none of that kind of talk. He set out to make people feel good about their country. And for a number of years, he succeeded with most Americans.

Reagan wore a conservative label, but in the choice of his closest advisers, he was a pragmatist. Of the three men who ran Reagan's White House, only one could be considered a "movement" conservative, Edwin Meese III, who had been chief of staff in Sacramento when Reagan was governor. Chief of Staff James Addison Baker III was the scion of a wealthy Texas family and had been educated at an eastern prep school and Princeton, an academic background not unlike that of his old friend George

Bush. Baker had been Bush's campaign manager when Bush was fighting Reagan for the 1980 presidential nomination, and conservatives were outraged when Reagan picked him as chief of staff. Michael Deaver, chosen to serve as Baker's deputy, was a California public relations executive. Deaver's loyalties were not to conservative politics, but to the Reagans, with whom he had a close association. Meese was the only member of the troika with conservative credentials, and his job as counsel to the president was, in many ways, the least important.

There is another example of Reagan's attitude toward conservatives. His political career had begun in 1965 when a group of extremely conservative California businessmen talked him into running for governor. These conservatives, Justin Dart, Holmes Tuttle, and Earl Jorgensen, among others, were called members of Reagan's kitchen cabinet, and most of them believed that they would serve as senior, if unofficial, advisers to the new president. There is no evidence that Reagan spent much time listening to them. He flattered them but ignored them in matters of substance, and soon the kitchen cabinet was no more.

Thus Baker, Deaver, and Meese were left in positions closest to the president, and Reagan usually listened to what they had to say. Baker, in particular, was an effective adviser. One day, angered by a leak to the press, Reagan ordered a wide-scale program of lie-detector tests for senior officials. Baker was at lunch when the president sent the order to Attorney General William French Smith. When Baker returned to the White House and learned what the president had done, he marched into the Oval Office and told Reagan that the lie-detector-test program was a terrible idea—bad for morale and bad politics. Reagan listened, picked up the phone, got the attorney general on the line, and ordered the program canceled.

Baker, Deaver, and Meese were an important part of Reagan's successful first term. (Reagan let the team slip away in his second term; unaccountably, he let Baker switch jobs with Treasury Secretary Donald Regan, who was a disaster as chief of staff. Deaver left to set up his own public relations and lobbying business and got in trouble with the law. He was subsequently convicted of perjury for lying to a congressional committee.)

Reagan brought important personal qualities to the presidency. He was charming, cheerful, and graceful under pressure. When he was wounded by an assassin during his first year in the White House, he joked with his doctors and apologized to his wife, saying he forgot to duck. Carter had made the work of the presidency look hard; Reagan made the job look easy. If the experts and the press thought he was short on knowledge of government, the public didn't care.

He was patriotic and optimistic, and his beliefs were fixed and easy to understand. The voters may have known that some of Reagan's oratory was flimflam; much of politics is just that. But people wanted a leader in the White House, and Reagan played that role masterfully. He said the things most Americans wanted to hear. Garry Wills, the historian, wrote, "We wanted him to fool us."

Most of Reagan's performance as president was carefully scripted; he was a superb political showman. But there was something else: plain good luck. Events not in his control had a way of breaking in his favor. The hostages in Iran were seized on Jimmy Carter's watch and released while Reagan was taking his oath of office. The price of imported oil had gone up disastrously during

Jimmy Carter's term; it dropped sharply during Reagan's, when OPEC reduced prices for the first time in its twenty-three-year history. When Reagan ran for reelection, the Democrats nominated Walter Mondale, Carter's vice president, a classic, old-fashioned liberal who ran a poor campaign. Against Mondale, Reagan was invulnerable. Reagan's biggest piece of luck came during his second term, when the Soviet Union began to change dramatically. Mikhail Gorbachev assumed power in 1985, two months after Reagan's second inaugural. Soon after, what Reagan had described as an "evil empire" was being transformed. Before Reagan left office, the Cold War came to an end. Ronald Reagan had his unlucky days, but they were outnumbered by his lucky ones.

Another reason for Reagan's popularity is that this Republican seems more like a Democrat. Political consultant David Sawyer called Reagan a "cultural Democrat." Reagan had been a liberal Democrat for much of his life, an admirer of Roosevelt who voted for Harry Truman in 1948. He didn't become a Republican until the early 1960s. Reagan grew up poor, a point of identification for millions of Democrats, and with nothing but his own talent, he made himself rich and famous. He was a union member who served for six terms as president of the Screen Actors' Guild. He is easygoing, genial, and has an Irish gift for storytelling—the kind of man, says Sawyer, you'd like to have a beer with. This is strange cultural garb for a Republican, but Reagan wore it with style.

His nice-guy image also brought him his Teflon skin. Nothing sticks to Teflon when it's on the frying pan, and, often, trouble didn't stick to Reagan when he was tossed into the fire. His image made him the envy of Washington. His administration would make a political blunder, or Reagan himself would botch something, and the president's popularity rating would remain high. People said he was able to cast a spell on the public, that his Teflon skin was a magic trick.

Not so. No politician can create such armament against trouble. If that were possible, they'd all do it. Teflon is a gift of the electorate, rarely bestowed. It is forgiveness. His Teflon skin didn't always work; it didn't protect him from a drop in popularity during the 1981–82 recession, and it didn't help him when the public decided that he'd been dealing with terrorists in the Iran-Contra scandals. But the Teflon was there most of the time. Some of it came from his own undeniable charm; more of it, in my view, came because Americans were tired of a series of failed presidents and wanted badly to see one succeed.

Reagan was like most presidents when he saw serious political trouble ahead: willing to do almost anything to avoid it. In the summer of 1986, it looked as though the Democrats might regain control of the Senate in the November elections. A dozen Republican senators in the farm states needed help. What would improve their chances? Selling grain to Russia. Reagan was fiercely anti-Soviet; the Red Army was still murdering women and children in Afghanistan. Secretary of State George Shultz furiously and publicly opposed the sale. Reagan nevertheless authorized hundreds of millions of dollars worth of subsidized grain to be sold to the Soviet Union. Because of the subsidies, Russians would pay less for the food than would Americans. The *Washington Post* said the administration wasn't selling wheat; it was buying votes. Reagan turned his back on principles he'd been advocating for years, and the subsidized grain was sent to the Soviet Union. In the end, it made no difference; the

Democrats recaptured control of the Senate in the fall. But it was a vivid demonstration of an important fact: Reagan's beliefs could be suspended by political necessity. Many presidents have done the same sort of thing, sometimes with useful results. The difference was that Reagan had described himself as a principled citizen crusader, not an opportunistic Washington politician.

The Reagan White House could be coldly calculating in its own political defense. In 1983, 241 American servicemen died in Beirut when an assassin drove a truck loaded with explosives into their barracks. The men, mainly U.S. Marines, had been sent there on a peacekeeping mission, and the "command picture," again, was murky, as it had been at Desert One. The dangers of Beirut were well known. Fifty people had been killed in a similar bomb attack on the American Embassy just six months before. Yet the U.S. Marines were in Lebanon on a "peacekeeping" mission. As part of this policy, they were not allowed to defend their perimeter with loaded weapons. The result was a ghastly massacre. It was clear that someone in command, at the Washington end or the Beirut end, had committed a hideous error.

But the president, as commander in chief, absolved his officers and took the blame upon himself. It was a mockery of the way military justice is supposed to work, and, of course, no one blamed Reagan personally for the needless deaths in Beirut.

There was, however, a political effect. Had there been courts-martial, the trials would have dragged on for months and been a prime story for the newspapers and television. Accused officers would have had the right to legal defense, and that would have taken more time and made more headlines. The trials and publicity would have dragged on during 1984, when the commander in chief was running for reelection. Closing the file on the Beirut massacre allowed the campaign to take place without distraction. By the time the presidential campaign got under way, the slaughter in Beirut had been out of the news for months.

It's been said that Reagan's success was based on the fact that he had been a movie star. That misses the point. His background as a film actor helped in his public appearances, of course, and, as actors do, he was careful to keep himself fit and active. On stage, he was an accomplished and guileful political performer. He was the oldest man ever elected president, but he turned his age into an advantage, using it as the source of endless, self-deprecating funny lines. In a 1984 presidential debate with Walter Mondale, he said, "I will not make age an issue in this campaign. I am not going to exploit, for political purposes, my opponent's youth and inexperience." Mondale was fifty-six, a former senator and vice president; Reagan was seventy-three. That triumphant one-liner, and many others as effective, was not accidental. Reagan took great care to polish his performances. It was said of him that he spent more of his time rewriting his speeches and public addresses than any other president. He was proud of his background in motion pictures. At the end of his second term, according to columnist George Will, "he said he sometimes wonder[ed] how presidents who have *not* been actors have been able to function."

All presidents, indeed, all successful politicians, are actors, good or bad, false or sincere. But Reagan brought an unusual mixture of character and talent to the White House. He combined country-boy simplicity about government with the polish of a professional actor. His acceptance of responsibility for the massacre in Beirut allowed him to play the kind of scene he believed in, the-buck-stops-here president, alone with his weighty responsibilities. At the same time it got him out of a tight political corner. Which was the real Reagan? *Both* were the real Reagan. That was his strength. Reagan the thespian was also Reagan the politician.

Reagan spent more years as a political activist and elected official than he had spent as an actor. For sixteen years he held two of the country's highest offices, governor of California and president of the United States. He spent six years running for the White House. He had a lax management style, he delegated too much, and he sometimes seemed bewildered by details, but underneath it all Ronald Reagan was a veteran, professional politician. He was not simply the creature of his writers or handlers. When there was a political job to do, he did it.

Appeasing the farm lobby was just one example. The federal farm-price support program had cost around $4 billion a year before Reagan became president; by 1986 it was $26 billion and rising. The elderly were politically organized; he tried once to curb social security benefits, backed off, and after that the benefits went up. Reagan was for free trade and against protectionism, but his administration set up barriers against a wide range of imported products, including steel, lumber, machine tools, automobiles, sugar, and textiles. Protectionism pleases its beneficiaries, but the consumer foots the bill when prices rise in protected industries. It has been estimated that consumers paid an extra $81 billion in 1989 because of trade restrictions. He had campaigned for a leaner government and specifically called for the elimination of the

Department of Education and the Department of Labor. These departments are supported by powerful constituencies, so they survived. He even established a new cabinet entity, the Department of Veterans Affairs. Any judgment on his record must be based on the fact that when it came to politics, he knew what he was doing.

He knew the full amount of his massive deficit spending, but he never asked the taxpayers to pay enough for the government programs he thought they ought to have. He wanted a huge military buildup. He wanted draconian cuts in domestic spending. But the Democrats, who controlled the House of Representatives, could be pushed only so far; they would not dismantle the domestic programs that were at the center of their party's appeal to the electorate. Reagan knew that, too. The result was a disastrous budgetary stalemate and rising deficits.

Some economists say the deficits matter; some say they are not in themselves a great danger. In 1983, the federal deficit stood at more than 6 percent of the GNP, which is extremely high; by the beginning of 1989, it had shrunk to about 3 percent, a more manageable level. The real problem posed by the deficit appears when it is seen as part of the enormous overall debt in the United States, government plus private debt run up by institutions and individuals. When debt is this high, when just paying the interest costs so many billions of dollars, a recession becomes more than a dip in the business cycle; it becomes a threat to the long-range health of the economy. A government that is deeply in debt has fewer weapons to fight a recession. Unemployment and lower earnings caused by a recession would make servicing the huge private debt more difficult. The wave of mergers, acquisitions, and corporation restructurings has saddled many with large amounts of debt that would be difficult to service in a recession. And no one can predict how foreign investors, with enormous holdings of U.S. government securities, might react to a serious economic downturn. A recession in the United States, because of the size of its economy and the enormity of its debt, would cause trouble everywhere in the world.

Perhaps the optimists are right, and the deficits by themselves don't matter. The problem is that they are not by themselves. The American economy today is like a car traveling down a road at ninety miles an hour with bald, worn tires. A blowout would be a disaster.

The huge government debt might have been averted if courage and dedication had been available. If the defense buildup had been less expensive, if the huge middle-class welfare state programs had been brought under control, if domestic spending had been cut drastically, the United States would have had a chance to get its books in order. Higher federal taxes would have helped, but nobody was in the mood for that, not the public, not the politicians, and certainly not the president, who used an old Clint Eastwood line, "Go ahead, make my day," when he challenged Congress to send him a tax-increase bill he could veto. In the end, nobody gave in; the Republicans got their programs, the Democrats held on to most of theirs, and both parties avoided the politically dangerous task of reining in the costs of the entitlement programs. Running up the deficits was the least unattractive political course. The Congress gave Reagan almost exactly what he asked for, year after year. The national debt tripled. Everyone in Washington knew what was happening. Each year's red ink was made public. With their eyes wide open, the White House and the Congress brought about the greatest explosion of public debt in the history of the United States. Reagan tried to say the Congress caused it, and many in the Congress said it was Reagan's fault, but for this flawed stewardship, for this wanton mismanagement of the nation's finances, they are both to blame. And, alas, so are the Americans who wanted more from the government than they were willing to pay for.

Government-by-borrowing produced prosperity, but it was a lopsided accomplishment. The rich got quite a lot richer, and the poor got decidedly poorer. Personal income for the affluent during most of the Reagan years increased 15 percent; for the poor, it declined 10 percent. In the aftermath of the 1981–82 recession, government figures showed a *simultaneous increase in both wealth and poverty.* No government figures had ever shown an increase in both directions, and that was the real story of the 1980s. The national savings rate remained catastrophically low during all but the last year of the Reagan administration. Foreign investors made up the difference as Americans went on spending and running up debt instead of saving. The rising tide of economic growth in the 1980s clearly did not lift all the boats, but it cast a kind of spell on a lot of Americans.

Many years ago, Budd Schulberg wrote a novel called *What Makes Sammy Run?* about a greedy, grasping Hollywood producer named Sammy Glick, one of the most repellent characters in American fiction. During the 1980s, Schulberg met a Harvard student who congratulated him on the book and who said Sammy Glick had become his role model. A stunned Schulberg wondered what was happening to the morals of young Americans if even one of them wanted to emulate the brutish, avaricious life of his antihero, Sammy Glick. In the 1980s, many did.

Sammy Glick would have enjoyed the decade. He would have understood the popularity of "Dynasty" and its dog-eat-dog characters. He would have sympathized with the cult of I-want-mine-now popular among the young. He would not have been surprised by the corruption on Wall Street, as inside traders went to jail. He would have reveled in the glitz and glitter. And he might have laughed at the increase in the number of people who fiddled with their taxes. Government surveys in the 1940s indicated that only 2 percent of taxpayers deliberately underreported their incomes. By 1985, the same surveys showed that 30 percent did so, mainly people in the upper-income brackets. It was a Sammy Glick kind of time, full of show, flash, and not a little crookedness. Money, what it could buy, how it could be flaunted, became important.

The owner of a fashionable restaurant in Orange County, California, told *Los Angeles* magazine a story about money and its importance. His restaurant sold wine by the glass, and one of the best-selling wines was an excellent California Chardonnay at $4 a glass. He bought so much of it that the winery gave him a large discount, and he dropped the price to $3.50. Same wine, lower price. Instantly, sales of the excellent Chardonnay dropped sharply. He raised the price to $4, and the wine again became his best-seller.

Money began to define groups of people: arbitrageurs, takeover artists, greenmailers, entrepreneurs. Magazines about money flourished. Businessmen wearing "power ties" took to meeting other businessmen for "power breakfasts." Salaries and bonuses for executives doubled and tripled. Sales of expensive foreign cars skyrocketed. "Whoever dies with the most toys wins" was regarded as a funny thing to say. DINKs appeared (Double Income, No Kids). So did WHOOPIES (Well-off Old People). And Yuppies (Young, Upwardly Mobile Professionals). There were jokes about Yuppie materialism ("Nuclear war? There goes my record collection. . . ."). There were Yuppie fashions—young women in tailored business suits, young men in horn-rims and suspenders. Bars opened that sold only water; for $3.50, you could buy a small bottle of Australian spring water. Yuppies "grazed" on light snacks instead of sitting down to meals. Certain exotic foods became fashionable. At Jack Murphy Stadium in San Diego, where the Padres play baseball, vendors in the stands began selling sushi. Mike Royko, columnist for the *Chicago Tribune*, asked if the Padre fans would now be singing,

Take me out to the ballpark,
Take me out to the game,
Buy me some sushi and I'll feel fine;
I might wash it down with a glass of white wine.

The truth, of course, was that the Yuppies and the white-wine sippers were vastly outnumbered by young Americans who were neither upwardly mobile nor professional. And a lot of them were working long hours pumping gas, pushing brooms, or frying fast-food hamburgers. The Harris poll reported that the workweek had increased 15 percent since 1973. But for most workers, hourly wages had gone to pieces: In 1973, a thirty-year-old male worker earned an average of $25,000 a year; by 1983, adjusted for inflation, that salary had dropped to $18,000. Home ownership in the 1980s declined for the first time since World War II. Higher housing costs and interest rates made home ownership almost impossible for the young, another part of the American dream shattered. But gloomy statistics were neither popular nor politically relevant during these years. The Yuppies and their rich elders dominated the scene. A financier named Ivan Boesky gave the 1986 commencement address at the University of California at Berkeley and told the graduates, "Greed is all right, by the way. I think greed is healthy." He later pleaded guilty to insider trading, but the message was appropriate for the time.

To understand the mood of the 1980s, it is necessary to consider the baby boomers. Seventy-six million people were born during the great postwar population surge called the baby-boom years, 1946 to 1964, a group that constitutes about one-third of the population today. The oldest are in their mid-forties, the youngest in their mid-twenties. A baby boomer who was born in 1946 has seen a lot of trouble in America. When John F. Kennedy was shot, our baby boomer would have been seventeen years old, the age when real political awareness begins; the defining political event of that young life was the murder of a handsome young president. Our baby boomer would have been fresh meat for the Vietnam draft in the late 1960s. By the time of the crippling inflation of the 1970s, when Jimmy Carter declared a national state of malaise, our baby boomer might have been married and struggling to raise a family; thirty-three years old when Iran seized the hostages; and thirty-six, with a few gray hairs showing, during the terrible recession of the early 1980s.

Baby boomers missed the America of the 1950s and early 1960s, the home-building, child-rearing optimistic America, with cheap home loans, good jobs, and the GI Bill to provide a college education. The baby boomers came of age in a world of working women, single-parent households, teenage pregnancies, fast-food meals, political assassinations, an unwinnable war in Asia, corruption in Washington, increasing foreign competition, crippling inflation, and a declining standard of living.

Things got better after the 1981–82 recession. Vietnam had faded from public concern (if not from the nation's movie screens). The hostages in Iran had been released. Unemployment was going down, and inflation had been licked. A popular president was proclaiming a Darwinian doctrine of individualism and entrepreneurship. In these circumstances, can this battered generation be blamed for an increase in materialism? For most of their adult lives, baby boomers had lived in a hard world of lowered expectations. When the sun came out, they enjoyed it. Reaganism, in a goofy evocation of the 1960s, urged them to "do their own thing," and they did.

The economic foundations for the greedy 1980s had been laid at least a decade before: the massive growth of pension funds playing the stock market (their money managers demanded a quick return on their holdings instead of long-range investment), the steady decline in the amount of money people saved, the rise in debt, and the deregulation of business that began under the Democrats and increased under the Republicans. The trend lines were clear before Reagan became president. What he did was to give them legitimacy.

Hugh Heclo, a professor of government at Harvard,

pointed out that "Reaganism urges Americans to dream dreams, but these are necessarily dreams of private advantage, not public accomplishment." There was a turning away from what Paul Goldberger, architecture critic for the *New York Times*, called "the public realm." Goldberger wrote:

Today in Los Angeles and Miami, in Boston and Chicago, as well as New York, we build great, shiny skyscrapers, but they are private, not public. We build enclosed arcades and shopping malls, but they, too, are private. Corporate office towers but not housing, private arcades but not parks: these choices stand as the symbols of our age. . . . If there is any legacy of the Reagan years, it is to have devalued completely the importance of the public realm and to have raised dramatically the value we place on the private realm, so much so that the public realm has almost ceased to have meaning.

When Goldberger penned that complaint in 1989, the United States was producing more goods and services than any other country and was in the seventh year of economic growth. Yet its government was not enlarging the public realm because there was neither the will nor the money to do so.

Federal support for nonprofit institutions in the social services and the arts dropped 20 percent during the 1980s, a loss of $30 billion in direct federal aid. The Reagan administration said volunteerism would take up the slack and asked corporations and individuals to double their charitable contributions. There was a rise in personal and corporate giving, but not enough to make up for a

$30 billion shortfall. Changes in the tax laws made giving more expensive for individuals, and a rise in corporate debt made it less easy for businesses to contribute.

One of the profit centers of these years was patriotism. Rambo movies were immensely popular. Sylvester Stallone and Chuck Norris were making hugely successful films about beating the Russians and avenging the American defeat in Vietnam.

In October 1983, the United States mounted a giant invasion of the small Caribbean island of Grenada. The White House said Grenada's government had been taken over by "a brutal group of leftist thugs" and that part of the mission was to rescue 1,100 Americans, mainly medical students, whose lives were in danger. The invasion was, in many ways, a tragicomedy. Grenada is an English-speaking island that welcomes tourists. The Reagan administration, and the president himself, had expressed concern over an airstrip being built there by Cubans because of its potential as a transshipment point for communist arms going to leftists in Nicaragua and rebels in El Salvador. The island was an open target for American intelligence, and, given what the president had said, a strategically important target.

The invasion, however, was an intelligence failure. Some of the planners, incredibly, did not know that Grenada is in the Atlantic time zone, not the Eastern time zone, and some of the air strikes were one hour late. When American troops set out to rescue the students, they had only tourist maps; military maps were unavailable. Later reports indicated that the students hadn't been in danger. The few hundred Cubans building the airstrip were not trained combat troops. And, as at Desert One in Iran in 1980, different units of the American armed forces couldn't talk to one another because their radios were on different frequencies. Another example of a flawed "command picture."

An armada of U.S. Navy ships participated in the invasion, and there was some hard fighting. Despite overwhelming American firepower, 133 American troops were killed or wounded. Cuban and Grenadan casualties were about half that number. The administration and the Department of Defense called it a great success. When it was over, the number of medals awarded by the Pentagon exceeded the number of U.S. servicemen in the operation.

Reagan justified the invasion by describing Grenada as a "Soviet-Cuban colony being readied as a major military bastion to export terror and undermine democracy. We got there just in time." The public agreed. More important, Grenada was seen as proof, to use Reagan's phrase, that "America was back." The days of American military humiliation, in Iran and in Lebanon, were over. It didn't matter that the United States had used a howitzer to kill a fly. It didn't matter that the invasion of Grenada might not have been necessary. What came through was the thrill of victory: America, at long last, had finally won one. The country rang with cheers.

The same kind of unconsidered patriotism appeared the following year at the Olympic Games in California. The United States had boycotted the 1980 games in Moscow. Four years later, the Soviet Union and most of the countries of Eastern Europe boycotted the games in Los Angeles. The subsidized, or more accurately, the paid professional athletes from the USSR and its East European satellites didn't show up, and they are among the toughest competitors in the world. As far as real competition was concerned, it wasn't a genuine Olympics.

But the games were an enormous public success. When American contenders won medals, and they won many, Americans in the stands roared, "USA! USA! USA!" When the games ended, some cities held parades to honor the American winners, and the crowds along the way repeated the patriotic chant heard in Los Angeles.

Were the American people ready to settle for sham triumphs in Grenada and at the Olympics? It seems that they were. The Republicans took full advantage of the public's mood and described Grenada and the Olympics as triumphs. One of the speakers at the Republican Convention in 1984 put the patriotic (and political) case for Grenada very clearly: "We have come a long way in four years—from the shame of Tehran to the brave rescue of American students in Grenada." And when he spoke, Reagan said, "Now it's all coming together. With our beloved nation at peace, we are in a springtime of hope for America. Greatness lies ahead of us. Holding the Olympic games here in the United States began defining the promise of this season." From time to time at the convention, groups of young Republicans, supervised by middle-aged party officials, would flow through the hall chanting, "USA! USA! USA!" America was back and standing tall.

The message of the 1984 convention was the essential message of Reaganism: The American experiment has been completed successfully, the nation's basic strengths are in place, the country can best be helped by those who help themselves, and no further tinkering need be done.

One of the great attractions of these propositions is that they require neither action nor pain. The great appeal of Reaganism was that it required so little from the electorate.

Hugh Heclo wrote, "Those who promise to solve problems by providing less government can expect to have an easier time dealing with the vicissitudes of public life than those pledged to use government actively for problem solving. Activism requires a constant supply of ideas and interventions, while limiting government requires mainly a consistent willingness to say no."

Among the many contradictions of the Reagan years is that despite his rhetoric about reducing the power of government, the public ended up wanting more of it. Public opinion polls toward the end of his second term showed that more than seven out of ten Americans wanted more government spending for health, housing, education, and help for the poor. In 1986, a Gallup poll found a sharp increase in those who believed that the federal government should "use its powers more vigorously." And while the youngest voters, men and women aged eighteen to twenty-four, identified with Reagan and the Republican party, they broke with him on social issues. Surveys showed that these young people held liberal views on civil rights and abortion.

Historian Arthur M. Schlesinger, Jr., a critic of Reaganism, argued that the number of Reagan appointees involved in ethical problems, those who were indicted or resigned under a cloud, exceeded the records for corruption and sleaze set by the Harding and Nixon administrations. And many Americans believe that standards of ethics in Washington declined while Reagan was president. Yet the University of Michigan's Center for Political

Studies found that overall trust in government almost doubled during the Reagan years. George Will observed that the public's increased trust in Washington is the salvation of the Democratic party.

What can be said of Reagan and the contradictions of his presidency? He spoke more harshly about the Soviet Union and spent more to arm against it than any other president. Yet he concluded his career with the first Soviet-American treaty to eliminate an entire class of nuclear weapons. With Mrs. Reagan on his arm, he strolled in Red Square. In his farewell address, he spoke of a "satisfying new closeness with the Soviet Union." It was a stunning ideological turnabout for a man who had built his career on passionate anticommunism, but for experienced Reagan watchers, it was not much of a surprise. Reagan had prospered in politics because he knew what pleased the electorate, and better relations with Moscow were enormously popular. Moreover, the USSR had become less belligerent under Mikhail Gorbachev, although Reagan's hard-line supporters thought it was too early to tell if the change was permanent.

When Reagan left the White House, a *New York Times*/CBS News poll reported that seven in ten of those polled supported his foreign policy, and 62 percent approved of his handling of the economy. The poll showed a mixed judgment on his presidency. More than half those surveyed said he had not told the truth about the Iran-Contra scandals. Almost half rejected Reagan's assertion that poverty had declined during his presidency (it had, but not by much). In the end, none of the negatives mattered: Reagan's approval rating when he left office was higher than that of any of his post–World War II predecessors. The oldest president in American history

had stayed the course for two terms, the first since Eisenhower to serve the full eight years. The country was not
at war. The state of the economy, aside from the budget
and trade deficits, was healthy. As the Reagan Enchantment came to an end, Reagan exited, smiling.

What must concern us now, however, is what was left
undone in the Reagan years.

The comptroller general of the United States is the senior
auditor in the federal government, appointed by the president to a fifteen-year term. He runs the General Accounting Office (GAO), a nonpartisan agency with 5,000 employees and an annual budget of $300 million. Charles A.
Bowsher was appointed by Ronald Reagan in 1981, and
under Bowsher's direction, the GAO has probably learned
more about the way Washington works than any other
arm of government.

In November 1988, two weeks after the election,
Bowsher gave President-elect George Bush an astonishing
report. It was an outline of what needed to be done to
correct the many areas of government neglected during
the Reagan years. The *New York Times* reported that "no
Comptroller General in the accounting office's 67-year
history had volunteered such advice to a President-elect
or, for that matter, so heavily implied criticism of an
outgoing president's management."

Some of the criticism was quite specific. The report told
Bush that urgent and immediate action was needed because the Reagan administration had ignored or exacer-
bated many pressing domestic problems and, in some
cases, created them. Across the entire spectrum of the
federal government's activities, the GAO found decay,

waste, and mismanagement. Funds had been cut so severely for research and data collection that government officials often didn't have enough information to make intelligent decisions. An example was the inability of the Transportation Department to determine whether the deregulation of airlines had reduced the safety of air travel. In general, the GAO reported, there was a need for more federal regulation of industries and activities that were deregulated during the Reagan years.

The State Department, said the report, had little idea of the value of properties it owned around the world and had allowed them to deteriorate through years of neglect. The Defense Department's stockpile of unneeded spare parts had tripled since 1980, but serious shortages of critical equipment, such as air-to-air missiles, remained. The GAO warned that if war were to break out, fuel and combat medical supplies might be exhausted "before the first major battle is concluded."

The report accused the Reagan administration of the mismanagement of public lands and stated it could find little evidence of success in efforts to reduce pollution of the environment. It noted that the Interior Department "must assume a more effective stewardship role" in the protection of public lands. And it said there had been failure to obey federal regulations on the storage or disposal of hazardous wastes. "After years of 'Fed-bashing' the new President needs to change course," Bowsher told Bush. The new president should abandon President Reagan's practice of denouncing federal agencies and civil servants because such talk makes it difficult for the government to "attract, motivate and retain committed people."

This was not an appraisal from the Democratic National Committee; it was the sober judgment of a nonpartisan agency held in high esteem in Washington, headed by a Reagan appointee.

The GAO report, along with other assessments of the condition of the United States in 1988, painted a grim picture of an America going to seed, its bridges and roads falling apart, its land scarred by dumps of untreated hazardous wastes, its national parks neglected, its savings-and-loan institutions bankrupt because of inadequate government supervision, its public housing deteriorating, its educational system in disrepair, its cities and suburbs scourged by drugs, its minority children impoverished, its prisons overcrowded, and its nuclear weapons plants in a state of shocking disarray.

Not all these problems are the fault of Ronald Reagan. Some of the bad management began years before he got to the White House. Congress and its many oversight committees and subcommittees must share the blame. The Democrats controlled the House of Representatives during his entire presidency and controlled the Senate for its last two years. But, because the president occupies such a central position, because the president is the leader of the government, because Ronald Reagan was so popular, and because he really didn't try to correct these problems during eight years in office, much of the responsibility must be his.

Part of the problem involved the Reagan administration's desire to get government off the backs of the people and to cut down the amount of reporting required of companies doing business with the government. Reducing excessive paperwork is a laudable goal, but the administration also cut back its ability to monitor its own activities. It got the government off the backs of the *government* by reducing the number of civil servants responsible for seeing that the books were properly kept and the rules followed. The White House Budget Office cut its staff nearly in half to set an example for other agencies. An official of the Justice Department lamented that the inspectors who checked the books of savings-and-loan institutions (S & Ls) were "a children's crusade" of inexperienced and underpaid examiners who failed to find discrepancies in the books kept by many S & Ls. The loss to the government in insurance payments to depositors was in the vicinity of $150 billion.

Bowsher of the GAO told a congressional committee, "When you look at what happened in the S & L crisis and look at the situation at H.U.D. and things like that, if we had proper systems, if we had the adequate financial reporting, if we had the right number of auditors to go out and check on this, we would have saved billions of dollars. In other words, we have been penny-wise and really pound-foolish here. It's a very scary situation for the federal government and the American taxpayer." The GAO estimated that the total losses caused by the government's inadequate oversight operations are in the range of $300 billion.

The costs inherited by the Bush administration are staggering. They include perhaps $200 billion for weapons plants, $20 billion for public housing, $5 billion for new prisons, $14 billion to clean up toxic wastes dumped by the Defense Department. They also entail more, perhaps far more, than $150 billion to rescue the S & Ls, $2 billion to restore the national parks, $22 billion to decontaminate hazardous waste sites, and $25 billion for a new air-traffic-control system. And, according to the Federal Highway Administration, at least $565 billion will be needed over the next twenty years to repair the interstate highway system.

The bill for all these costs comes to more than a trillion dollars. Beyond these urgent and immediate tasks stand other multi-billion-dollar obligations: the war on drugs, help for Americans with no health insurance, and desperately needed improvements in education.

The indebtedness of the government has limited the power and influence of the United States in world affairs. At the end of Reagan's presidency, American's foreign aid program was smaller than Japan's; the Japanese were winning friends—and contracts—with a greatly expanded program of foreign assistance. There was no large-scale American government program available to help Poland and Hungary join the capitalist world. When the countries of Eastern Europe broke free of communism, Moscow stood aside, but Washington had run out of money. The Cold War ended not with a bang but with deficits.

The United States even has trouble meeting some of its obligations to international financial organizations. In the summer of 1989, Congressman Lee Hamilton put a question to Treasury Secretary Nicholas Brady: "Does this mean that the baton of leadership is going to be passed to other nations?" Brady replied, "I must admit that from the point of view of the Treasury it is a source of some embarrassment in world-wide forums not to be able to come up with our agreed-to subscriptions to the World Bank and other multilateral institutions. I don't think we have a passing of the baton yet, but it is a serious worry."

A serious worry, indeed, and not just in international forums. The United States is in danger of losing its position as number one in the world. Its baton of leadership may actually be passed. For a number of reasons, that would be a colossal tragedy.

It is not posturing to say that the world needs a United States operating at full power. The West Europeans are not unified enough to provide leadership in the West. The Japanese are too unified and too insular to provide leadership in the East. A leaderless world would be a dangerous world.

The worst tragedy would be here at home, made all the more bitter because it needn't have happened. The paradox of America today is that we know what needs to be done to correct our faults. We know what sacrifices must be made, what energies are needed to keep our strength from slipping away. Yet few of our political leaders are willing to ask us to act and few are willing to talk plainly and honestly about the emergency facing the country.

Unless action is taken now, the task of rebuilding America will fall to our children and to their children. And by the time they take charge, it may be too late to hold on to the baton of leadership.

PART THREE

How Do We Get Out of This Mess?

Ihere are two popular views of America's future, and both of them are wrong.

One is that the United States should stay the course, work on its problems, and slowly but steadily grow out of its difficulties. This argument cites the colossal capacity of the American economy, the nation's vast resources, and its political and military power in the world. The United States may be going through a difficult time, but its sheer size will keep it healthy and ahead of its competitors. With confidence in the future, all will be well.

The second view is that the power of the United States is in gradual, ineluctable decline. The world is changing, and centers of power are shifting. The Cold War rivalry that dominated international affairs for four decades has exhausted both the United States and the Soviet Union. High technology, vital to the country's economy and defense and the key to its economic well-being, is being taken over by better-financed Japanese and Europeans. Commerce has replaced ideology. The best course for Americans is to accept the inevitable and manage the country's gradual decline.

The problem with the growth scenario is that America's problems of debts and deficits have not been solved in the course of more than seven years of economic growth. The federal deficits may get *larger* in the 1990s. The trade deficit remains unacceptably high and it may increase. This unusually long period of peacetime prosperity has not improved the country's bankrupt educational system, bettered the plight of its poor, or made it more competitive. Staying the course, betting on what has been called the "puberty economics theory of growth," will not do the job.

The problem with the scenario that describes America in decline is that there is nothing inevitable about that decline, just as there is nothing inevitable about Japanese or European dominance. The European Community is working to turn itself into a single commercial market, a goal it may reach in the early 1990s. But genuine political cohesion of the twelve member countries, a truly coordinated entity, remains a dream of the European Community bureaucrats in Brussels. Recent events may make this goal even more difficult to reach. The transformation of Eastern Europe and its new economic potential is redrawing the map from the Baltic to the Mediterranean. The vision of a Western Europe free of frontiers by 1992 has been clouded and made more complex by the liberation of Eastern Europe.

Further, Japan is beginning to undergo changes that will make it less competitive: Its population is aging, its young people are demanding an easier life, and its huge trade surpluses are decreasing. The Japanese are beginning to enjoy the fruits of their labor. In 1989 alone, 10 million Japanese spent more than $20 billion on foreign travel, a record number and a record amount. Japan will continue to be an awesome economic power, but there is little chance that it will replace the United States as the leading political and military power in the Pacific. In fact, the Japanese themselves are deeply worried that the leadership of the United States may falter. And the Japanese reject the idea that America is in decline: In a Harris poll taken in the autumn of 1989, only one Japanese in five believed that the United States was on an irreversible path of social and economic decline.

It is possible that the USSR could mount a challenge to American leadership sometime in the next century. Perestroika and glasnost may someday allow the Soviet Union to utilize its great natural resources effectively and take its rightful position as a world power. As of today, however, the evidence points toward continued poverty and political turmoil. And the political instability of this heavily armed nuclear power is another argument for the continuation of American military and political leadership.

America's present inadequacies are not the inevitable product of the ebb and flow of history. They are problems created by drift and inattention, which can be solved by work and dedication. They are challenges to a free people who control their national policy through a tested and durable electoral process. The citizens of the United States can create an American renaissance; the tools are in their hands. The inventory of American strength is immense: Its ideology remains the most appealing in the world; its huge free market, bound by a common language and open interstate borders, is the envy of other trading blocs (the goal of the European Community is to become a group of *united states*). The American network of military and diplomatic alliances, its primacy in world trading and economic institutions, give it enormous influence.

America's decline is not written in the stars, but complacency will not preserve its strength. So, it is a third view of America's future that concerns us here. It is time to get to work.

If the United States is able to recognize the gravity of its peril, if the American people, with all their skill and energy, can be made to face their problems directly, the future can be bright and secure. There is talent and intelligence enough to do the job. The job will require sacrifice and commitment, leadership and plain talk, and a renovation of some American institutions.

In our intensely political country, change must begin with politics. For more than fifty years, the central argument in American politics has been about what I call the zoo and the jungle. Is America a liberal zoo, or is it a conservative jungle? If it is a zoo, the government must guarantee that the inhabitants are cared for from the cradle to the grave. This argument makes the government the keeper of the zoo—the provider of education, medical care, employment, housing, and a comfortable retirement. Franklin Roosevelt's New Dealers in the 1930s, responding to the Great Depression, set most of these policies in motion. Democratic and Republican presidents, from Truman to Carter, kept them in place and some, including Eisenhower and Nixon, extended the responsibilities of government as the zookeeper.

During the Reagan years, the jungle theory had its day. Mr. Reagan was elected on a promise of less government involvement; he would get the government off the backs of the people. Some of his conservative supporters believed the only proper role for government was the defense of the country. Private enterprise could deliver the mail, run the schools, and heal the sick. It was a Darwinian belief that the survival of the fittest benefits rich and poor alike because it creates a bounteous prosperity. For those who could not help themselves there would be a "safety net" of government support, a small zoo surrounded by a large, vibrant, exciting, and productive jungle.

It didn't work out that way, of course. The safety net had holes in it. The gap between the rich and the poor is now the widest in forty years. At the same time, the function of government as zookeeper wasn't greatly reduced. Millions of Americans enjoy being cared for. They are largely of the middle class and therefore politically powerful. One of the significant components of the government's burden of debt is the continued growth of entitlement programs, such as social security and Medicare, that serve middle-class voters.

It is time to end this half century of debate about the zoo and the jungle. The liberal zoo made sense when the country was on its knees during the Great Depression. The conservative jungle argument had its most forceful presentation during the Reagan years. Neither has much potency in today's world. Neither the liberals nor the conservatives have an appealing message these days. Most of the traditional liberal goals were achieved by the end of the 1960s. There has been only one Democratic president since 1969, Jimmy Carter, and he was propelled to victory by Nixon's Watergate crimes, not by an attractive liberal program. Carter wasn't very liberal and lasted for only one term. Similarly, the energy is gone from conservative Republicanism. Without the cause of anticommunism, Republicans have become a party searching for a theme. Democrats and Republicans, liberals and conservatives, have run out of great national objectives.

Yet there is one great and urgent political matter on the nation's agenda: the maintenance of American world leadership. But in this struggle, traditional liberal or conservative nostrums will not suffice; fighting the old left-right battles will not help; trench warfare between Democrats and Republicans in Washington will not do. What the country needs from its elected officials is a recognition of the emergency and action taken to overcome it. Sterile ideological labels of the past should be abandoned, as the United States girds for the competitive battles of the twenty-first century.

In a world of increasing economic challenge, what's liberal about giving American children an education as good as that provided to Japanese children? Is it conservative or liberal to make American workers as healthy as Canadians or West Germans? Is safety in the workplace only a liberal idea pushed by labor unions, or does safety make sense if American productivity is to increase? Day care is not a women's issue; it is a national issue, vital to a country in which more and more jobs are held by women. Getting people out of poverty and providing children with a decent education are now basic weapons in the battle to make the United States a competitive player in the world. Would Japan put up with a work force that was at 80 percent of its strength because of impoverished, undernourished, and ill-educated workers? Would Western Europe allow its inner cities to be abandoned to decay? Can incentives for more research and development or proposals for greater government-business partnerships be called liberal or conservative? The old political designations are now out of date. Under eight years of a conservative Republican president, the United States assumed a mountain of debt. The tax-and-spend Democrats won't call for a needed increase in taxes. The old days are over. There is a compelling need for a new vocabulary of American politics, more pragmatic and less partisan, free of the ideological divisions of the past. We must put aside liberalism and conservatism in favor of cooperation and action.

Unfortunately, Washington hasn't learned that lesson. The only clear message the Congress has sent to the voters is that its members place the highest priority on getting reelected. Nothing else seems to matter. Voters must be placated at all costs, which means that no one is willing to run any risks. This malady now affects nearly all elected officials. The president calls for bold new programs but does not say where the money for them will come from. He is not responsible for raising the funds. Obsolete military bases must be closed; the Congress does it by passing a law that makes no member personally responsible for the closing of a base.

On Capitol Hill, they smile and call these schemes to avoid accountability the "Immaculate Conception" process. No human being is responsible. Risk-free politics is one way of ensuring reelection, but it is the worst possible legislative strategy for a country in acute need of innovative leadership and political reform.

The reform should begin with the system used to choose the president. Presidential campaigns last too long, cost too much, and too often produce poor candidates. Every four years, the American voter is subjected to ten months of banal hucksterism, a farrago of tasteless advertising and shallow rhetoric. The latest example was the 1988 contest between George Bush and Michael Dukakis. The United States was in deep trouble in 1988, but instead of a debate on what could be done to help the country, the voters got cheap irrelevancies from Bush about Dukakis's prison-furlough program and his alleged failure to clean up Boston Harbor. What the voters saw in the flag-draped Bush campaign was a political operation as free from real issues as Ronald Reagan's had been four years before. What the voters got from Dukakis was a punch-drunk performance as inept as Walter Mondale's had been four years before. And so it goes, presidential election after presidential election. Isn't there a better way?

What Theodore H. White called "the making of the president" has become the merchandising of the president. We have allowed a system to be created that relies on the mass marketing of candidates. Every election year, for month after dreary month, advertising pours out of television sets, beginning with the Iowa caucuses in January, lasting until the election in November. Dozens of presidential candidates run in dozens of primaries, paying millions for television advertising. Pat Robertson spent $30 million in the 1988 primaries. He has since disappeared from view, another political outsider who came from nowhere and tried unsuccessfully to manipulate the primary system.

Primary elections and party caucuses should be abolished. It can be done. It is within the power of the political parties to change their procedures. There is nothing in the Constitution that requires primary elections. The best reform would be to let party professionals and elected officials choose the party's standard-bearer for the fall campaign. It sounds like heresy, but the power to choose presidential *candidates* needs to be taken from the people. Voters in primaries are not like voters in general elections; too often, primary voters are zealous, single-issue partisans. They will drive through howling blizzards to vote for a candidate who supports gun control—or for a candidate who's against it. The number of people who bother to vote in primaries is small: Why should they be allowed to choose two presidential candidates who are then presented to the rest of us?

Primaries are a recent political invention. In the beginning, starting in 1796, presidential candidates were chosen in party caucuses held by members of Congress. In the 1830s, parties began making their choices at national nominating conventions. Under both systems, those who did the choosing were career politicians. It was not until after World War II that the primary election system came to life, and not until the 1970s that it became the only path to the presidency.

In 1980, Jeane Kirkpatrick, then a professor at Georgetown University, proposed that primaries be abolished. She proposed a system under which the choice would be made only by elected officials and party leaders. Austin Ranney, the political scientist, wrote, "In the old smoke-filled room days, the people who really chose the presidential nominee were people who knew the candidates and saw them in action and had some idea of what they were like." Ranney doesn't think that a return to the smoke-filled room, in which a few bosses make the decision, would be possible. He does believe that political leaders should be the deciding influence at the national parties' nominating conventions.

The power to choose presidential candidates should be returned to the national party conventions, and the delegates to the conventions should be seasoned political professionals. Austin Ranney made a key point when he argued that choosing a candidate requires the experience of a political pro and that personal knowledge of a candidate's strengths and weaknesses is vital. Gary Hart was a powerful presidential candidate. He destroyed his candidacy because of personal mistakes. Had he not stumbled, he might have won enough delegates in the primaries to get his party's nomination, and perhaps win the presidency. But at a convention of professionals, would Hart have survived the judgment of his peers, who knew him?

Political professionals are in the best position to judge the electability of candidates and their fitness to serve as president. The press, however vigilant, is less qualified for this task. And least qualified of all are the delegates, who are too often ordinary citizens chosen in the tumult of a primary election, selected because of their loyalty to a candidate rather than their political experience.

Under today's system, candidates win blocs of delegates in the primaries. When the delegates finally arrive at the convention, they have already been pledged to candidates, and the candidate with a majority of the delegates picks up the nomination that he won in the primary states often months before. In 1988, more than a month before the Democratic Convention, Michael Dukakis had won enough delegates in the primaries to clinch the nomination. The Republicans held their convention in August; George Bush had locked up his nomination in March. The convention process, as it stands today, is arithmetical but not political.

If the parties had real national conventions, the delegates would sit in sovereign assembly with unlimited authority. The choice of the presidential nominee would be completely in their hands. Delegates at a genuinely open convention could call candidates to appear for further questioning or ask them to make a speech. Opposing candidates could be asked to debate. The whole thing would be messy and political and could go on for a long time. There might be many ballots. The result would be a marvelous show. The television networks would follow every move.

Such a system would produce more electable candidates, not darlings of the right or the left or candidates who won the most delegates in the dice games of the primaries. A convention of seasoned politicians would pay less attention to ideological purity and more to a candidate's chances of winning. That would create real contests for the presidency in the fall campaigns, with two candidates chosen for their electability, each able to appeal to that great mass of centrist voters who represent the heart of the American political system. If there were no primaries, there would be no need for television advertising in the primary states and no need for candidates to beg for money to put the ads on the air. And abolishing the primaries would shorten the length of the presidential process from ten months to four. Shorter presidential campaigns might get more people involved in the process and increase voter turnout. Dare we think that better presidential campaigns might even get voters to stop splitting their votes, electing Republican presidents and Democratic congresses? Government divided by party is bad government. If either party controlled both the White House and the Congress, we would at least have one party to blame. That's the way the country used to work.

It is my view that the party that returns to the open

convention will create such interest and drama, so much excitement and suspense, that its chances of winning the November election will be greatly enhanced. And if one party does it and wins, the other party will do it four years later.

Television can play an important role at an open convention. When the networks began to show the conventions to a national audience in 1952, a symbiotic relationship was established between the audience and the politicians. Millions of viewers watched savage arguments over party platforms, dramatic confrontations over delegates' credentials, even multiple-ballot roll-call votes. It was sensational television, but it was also a lesson in American politics watched by millions. Important national concerns—civil rights, taxes, poverty, foreign policy—were debated on live television. The most colorful characters in American politics became familiar figures across the country. Coverage began about a week before the convention assembled and lasted until the last speech was made. Much of it was pure magic, and out of it came a national awareness of what American politics was all about.

Gavel-to-gavel coverage lasted about twenty years. At the beginning, it was easy for the networks because they had nothing else to show in the daytime and nothing as exciting to show in the evening. But over the years, the attitude of the networks and the politicians changed. The networks had other competitive pressures for daytime and prime-time ratings. And the political parties began to sanitize their conventions, which took all the fun out of them and ended up boring the audience. *Sic transit gloria mundi.* The greatest civics lessons in American history had been turned into deodorized coronations.

What is needed in America today is a return to a system of electing presidents that gets people *engaged*. There used to be ardor in politics. On Saturday nights in bars, political arguments would lead to fistfights. That kind of thing is part of the lusty tradition of American politics, but it hasn't happened since the 1960s. The fun went out of it when Johnson ran against Goldwater in 1964, and we haven't had a really inspiring presidential election since. Politics has become a big-money game, about as enjoyable as a leveraged buyout. We used to have marvelous presidential elections: Truman's surprise victory over the supposedly unbeatable Thomas E. Dewey; an elegant Adlai Stevenson running vainly against a majestic Dwight Eisenhower; Kennedy and Nixon's memorable struggle in 1960. Can't we get the thrill back? The sense of working together toward a common goal?

Today's elections, saturated with name-calling and attack advertising, have become more gladiatorial than political. The combatant who is still alive at the end is served up to us as our new president, governor, senator, or member of Congress. It happened in 1988 and it will happen again in 1992. Roger Ailes, who produced the negative Bush campaign of 1988, has been quoted as saying, "If you didn't like 1988, you'll *hate* 1992."

What the voters need are candidates who stand for new programs, policies, and leadership; candidates who can give people the sense that their votes will actually make a difference; candidates responsive not to people's fears, but to their dreams.

There was a thrilling moment in 1961 when President Kennedy told a joint meeting of the Congress, "I believe that this nation should commit itself to achieving the goal, before this decade is out, of landing a man on the moon and returning him safely to earth. No single space project in this period will be more exciting, or more impressive to mankind, or more important to the long-range exploration of space; and none will be so difficult or expensive to accomplish."

Today, what could be more exciting, more impressive, than rescuing the United States from the peril it faces? Such an undertaking, of course, would be difficult and expensive. That may be why our recent presidents have avoided setting bold challenges before the electorate. It is no longer "good politics" to ask Americans to suffer or bleed, even a little, for an important national goal. Nixon and Ford didn't do it. Carter lectured Americans on their shortcomings. Reagan told them they didn't have to do anything except sit back and enjoy life. Reagan turned Kennedy around; the message was, Ask not what you can do for your country, but what your country can do for you.

It's been a long time since the American people have been presented with an inspiring national challenge, something into which they could sink their very capable teeth. There is, however, every reason to believe they would respond, if someone would tell them in plain language what needs to be done, and guarantee that the effort would be shared equally.

That person needs to be the president, but the president can't do it alone. The Congress shares the power, but in the United States today, the Congress has lost its moral authority. Its members are viewed by the public as overpaid, underworked, in thrall to lobbyists and special interests, anxious only to hold on to their safe seats. That perception, of course, is not true: Many members of Congress are respectable, hardworking lawmakers. But it is the perception that counts, and the public holds the Congress, and politicians in general, in low esteem. A recent survey taken for the American Medical Association found that "voters see an ever-widening gulf between the values and attitudes of politicians and the values and attitudes of themselves, their families and their neighbors." By two to one, people polled for that study said their government leaders are less trustworthy than they were ten or fifteen years ago.

Do the American people now operate on the assumption that corruption is endemic on Capitol Hill? A century ago, Mark Twain said that members of Congress were the only "distinctly American criminal class," which may have had more relevance then than it does now. But the resignation of the Speaker of the House in 1989 tells us something about the public's attitude. There was little public concern when Jim Wright resigned during an ethical scandal. The resignation was, in truth, a national calamity. The Speaker of the House is third in line for the presidency, after the vice president. No Speaker had ever been forced to resign. But instead of asking what the country was coming to, instead of clamor and alarm, the public accepted the resignation almost as a matter of course, as though ethical lapses on Capitol Hill were an everyday occurrence. They aren't, but the important thing was that the public reacted as though they were. Perhaps *that* response should make us ask what the country's coming to.

The negative reaction to an increase in congressional pay is one piece of evidence that large sections of the public have lost faith. The pay raise was justified, but what the public saw was privilege and the easy life. It saw members of Congress enjoying an array of expensive perks, from subsidized haircuts to free health clubs, from free long-distance phone service to parking privileges at any open curb space in the capital (except in front of fire hydrants, please). Congressional life insurance policies are paid for, in part, by the taxpayers, and pensions are tied to inflation, which means that many retired members get more from their pensions than they got in their salaries. Other benefits include overseas junkets paid for by the government or by special-interest groups. In 1990, the Congress said it would need $2.7 billion to run its affairs, which comes to about $5 million for every member. And, by law, no other agency of government can interfere with the Congress's own budget.

There's a lot of money sloshing around in the corridors of Congress. For example, leaving it can be extremely profitable. A congressman resigned in 1989 and pocketed $345,000 in unused campaign funds. He just took the money, which was perfectly legal. The law allows members of the House who were elected before 1980 to convert to their personal use any money left in their campaign chests when they retire. When John Tower of Texas retired from the Senate, he picked up $445,000 in surplus campaign funds. At the beginning of 1989, 191 members covered by the law had squirreled away a total of $39 million in campaign funds. A new ethics law repealed the keep-the-loot provision, but the repeal doesn't take effect until 1993. And what may happen in 1992? A number of senior House members may retire and go home with the swag. There was speculation that the chairman of the House Ways and Means Committee, Dan Rostenkowski, might be among them. His campaign bank account contains more than a million dollars.

Retirement or death is about the only way people leave the House these days. The House has become a citadel of incumbency. In the past ten years, only eighty-eight incumbent members who sought reelection failed to win. The House has built a wall around itself to keep challengers out, which is not the way the House was designed to work. When the Constitution was written, its framers thought of the House of Representatives as the legislative body closest to the public's pulse, most responsive to the country's changing needs. They even considered one-year terms for House members, but roads were so bad and travel to home districts so difficult in 1787 that the proposal was dropped in favor of two-year terms. The framers wanted the House to be constantly renewed by new members with fresh ideas. Today, the House has locked its doors to new blood. The turnover rate of seats in the House of Representatives is only slightly higher than the turnover rate in Britain's House of Lords, where only death can create a vacancy. The rate of return for incumbents in the elections of 1988 was 98 percent. The U.S. Senate is almost as safe for its incumbent members; 85 percent of those who sought reelection in 1988 were returned.

It must be said that members of Congress work hard to keep their jobs. According to Congressman Guy Vander Jagt, the ratio of outgoing to incoming mail in congressional offices is 100 to 1, and much of that outgoing mail is political propaganda paid for with funds from the U.S. Treasury, sent unsolicited to unwary voters. Senator Alan Cranston used $4.8 million in public money to send newsletters to constituents in California in the ten months preceding his reelection in 1986. Members of Congress have used federal funds to buy mailing lists to reach ever-wider groups of voters with expensive mailings subsidized by the taxpayers' money. They have at their service, free of charge, the power of radio and television. When the House is not in session, members use its television production facilities to make videotapes that are sent to television stations in their home districts for use on news programs. The tapes show a member making an impassioned speech in the House chamber. What the tapes do not show is that the member is usually the only person in the chamber.

If such a high percentage of congressmen and senators enjoy what amounts to lifetime tenure, we have a right to expect them to use their experience to pass wise laws and guarantee that the laws are enforced. But that is not always the case. The many congressional committees watching over the S&L industry failed to prevent the most costly mismanagement in American history, for which the public must pay a staggering price. The Heritage Foundation calculated that eighty-four different congressional committees and subcommittees, controlled by Democrats, had some sort of oversight responsibility for the Department of Housing and Urban Development. Yet nobody seemed to notice that, over a period of years, HUD was handing out billions of dollars in favors to Republican politicians. The watchdogs on these eighty-four congressional committees and subcommittees seem to have been asleep when the looting of HUD took place.

Maybe they were watching the Pentagon. Defense Secretary Richard Cheney reported that 107 committees and subcommittees have some jurisdiction over the Defense Department. More than 400 written inquiries from Congress and 2,500 telephone calls from congressional offices are received at the Pentagon *every working day*—more than 750,000 inquiries a year. Each day that Congress is in session, Defense Department officials spend an average of fourteen hours testifying. The cost of this reporting to Congress is enormous, and its usefulness is dubious. In 1988, procurement scandals at the Pentagon made headlines. The scandals, however, were discovered not by 107 committees and subcommittees but by the Defense Department itself.

The Congress sometimes has difficulty passing wise laws. When it found itself unable to reduce the deficit, it concocted a bizarre scheme called The Gramm-Rudman-Hollings Act that was the legislative equivalent of a dieter wiring his jaws together so he can't eat: If the deficit couldn't be reduced through compromise and negotiation, cuts in government spending would be made automatically. Senator Rudman called it "a bad idea whose time has come." Automaticity is supremely attractive to members of Congress; it means that no individual member is responsible for an unpopular action. The Supreme Court ruled that making these mindless, automatic cuts was unconstitutional, but in modified form, Gramm-Rudman lives on as a shield against responsibility. Both the president and Congress find it useful, but the deficits continue to increase. Senator Ernest Hollings, an original sponsor of the law, called it "the fraud that we have all perpetrated on the American people."

Can anything be done to make the Congress perform more efficiently? There is. The public, the press, and civic organizations should demand that the wall that protects incumbents be torn down. The reform should start with money. A way must be found to cut down or eliminate the cash that political action committees give to members of Congress. Three-fourths of the PAC contributions go to incumbents, giving them overwhelming advantages over their challengers. In the 1988 elections for House seats, incumbents had approximately $200 million in campaign funds, while their challengers had $36 million, according to Common Cause, the public-interest group.

The Republicans have a strong interest in making it easier for challengers to run against incumbents: Most incumbents are Democrats, who outnumber the Republicans in both houses of Congress. Democrats regard most Republican proposals for campaign reform as a threat to their dominance. When President Bush proposed a package of campaign-reform measures, the Democratic National Committee chairman called it "the fat cat protection act of 1989." But there is merit in the president's plan. Bush wants to eliminate PACs sponsored by corporations, unions, and trade associations, which would be a healthy move, although possibly a violation of the First Amendment. He wants political parties to be able to double the amount of money they can contribute to candidates for the House and the Senate, which would strengthen the parties. The president wants members of Congress to pay postage for their mass mailings, and he wants greater public disclosure of campaign contributions.

Bush did not recommend public financing of congressional campaigns, which is ironic, because after he won his party's nomination, he got $46 million in public financing to run for president. My own feeling is that public financing for congressional campaigns is a *good* idea whose time has come. A fixed amount of public campaign money would slow down the flood of political advertising that pollutes the airwaves every two years. It would allow challengers and incumbents to contest on a level playing field because it would erase the enormous financial advantages that incumbents with multi-million-dollar war chests now enjoy. Pete Wilson spent nearly $13 million in California in 1988 to defend his seat in the Senate. Many members of Congress now spend more time fund-raising than legislating, and all of them find it a vile chore and a constant embarrassment. Common Cause reported that senators preparing to run for reelection in 1990 were raising money at the rate of *$145,000 a day*. The time has come to take the tin cup out of the political process, get the special-interest contributors out of the game, and let the taxpayers foot the bill.

A Congress not besotted with fund-raising and open to new blood and new ideas would be more responsive to the country's needs and, perhaps, more courageous in meeting them. New members would bring it closer to the people. If changes are not made, the people themselves may make them. The *Wall Street Journal* reports that moves are under way in several states to limit the tenure of lawmakers because of criticism of entrenched incumbents. Ralph Nader, the activist who is tireless and relentless in his campaign against congressional privilege, wants to organize a "Campaign of Citizens" that will demand a limit of twelve years of congressional service. This is not, perhaps, a wild idea; the law already limits a president to two consecutive four-year terms.

Achieving a better Congress and a better way of nominating presidential candidates are objectives within the grasp of the American people. The reforms I have outlined do not call for tinkering with the Constitution. They are within the power of our political parties, our elected officials and, ultimately—ourselves. The United States does not have to amend its Constitution to change its ways.

But its government must change the way it does business. The United States faces great perils, and it has only a decade or so, a window of opportunity of perhaps ten years, in which to prepare for the intense competition it will face in the next century.

Part of the problem is that the doctor hasn't given the patient a complete report on the illness. The president should give the American people a full description of the country's situation, of its strengths and its weaknesses. George Bush has addressed some of the problems, and his cabinet is working on others, but he ought to appear before the nation and talk plainly about what needs to be done. People will not rally by themselves, and while most Americans feel that things are not right, they don't have the details and they don't have an agenda for change. Only the president has the stature to set the facts before the people. Only the president can command the attention of the nation. He must explain, persuade, and lead. An appearance before a joint meeting of the House and the Senate would be the way to begin.

The president should bring some Democrats into the White House, as a signal to the country that these are extraordinary times that demand extraordinary actions. If the next president is a Democrat, he should bring in some Republicans. Some names of Democrats come easily to mind: Harold Brown, who was Carter's secretary of defense, an expert on technology; Cyrus Vance, a former secretary of state who served several presidents; former Senator Abraham Ribicoff, a shrewd observer of Congress. There are many others in business and academe. Franklin Roosevelt brought Republicans into his cabinet during World War II. The result was not only better government; Roosevelt sent a signal to the American people that winning the war was more important than was politics. Mr. Bush's prominent Democrats need not be cabinet officers, but the president would be well served by a council of wise men from both parties, and the country would get the message that the White House is serious about what is, in fact, a national emergency.

Most voters these days are against raising taxes. The president says, "Read my lips, no new taxes." Many experts say that some taxes must be increased. Who's right? Everybody's right, but in different ways. George Bush is right, for narrow political reasons: Taxes are unpopular. It is understandable that voters are against them; they were conditioned in the Reagan years to pay eighty cents in federal taxes for every dollar of government services. That ran up a debt of almost as much money as was needed to finance World War II. It was an addictive experience. Voters are hooked on low taxes. And, finally, the experts are right when they say that tax increases are needed because spending cuts alone cannot effectively reduce the deficit. That is the most important judgment of all.

Among those calling for higher taxes are former presidents Gerald Ford and Jimmy Carter, who are cochairmen of a bipartisan group called American Agenda that recommended higher taxes on beer, wine, cigarettes, and gasoline. The chairman of the Federal Reserve System,

Alan Greenspan, believes that reducing the deficit is so important that it must be done even if it means raising taxes. And the former chairman of the Federal Reserve, Paul Volcker, as tough-minded as they come, said in 1989, "I don't think you can argue that from an economic standpoint you would do grave damage to the economy by raising any or all taxes by relatively modest amounts."

Large revenue gains flow from relatively modest increases in taxes. Every extra penny in the gasoline tax generates $1 billion. A 5 percent value-added tax, a sort of national sales tax, would bring in perhaps $100 billion a year. And it could be adjusted so it didn't overburden the poor. *The Economist*, a magazine that is conservative in its economic views, says that a 1.5 percent increase in taxes would bring the deficit down to a manageable level in four years.

None of these proposals deals with the top rate of the income tax, which is lower in the United States than in any of its competitor countries. The top rate is 56 percent in West Germany and 50 percent in Japan. In the United States it is about half that. Do the Japanese and the West Germans know something we don't know?

There is a compelling case to be made for more government revenue, whether it's a tax on beer or an increase in the income tax. The federal deficit must be reduced. And there are essential programs that must be funded if the United States is to keep its competitive edge. From $50 billion to $100 billion a year could be raised in new tax revenues without harming our $5 trillion economy.

Alice M. Rivlin, the former head of the Congressional Budget Office, proposed that some of the new revenue be

given directly to state governments. Many state governments are far more effective than they once were; state
legislatures are now more responsive to the public's needs.
Many of the states could spend the money more wisely
than the U.S. Congress. Rivlin argues that if $35 billion
to $50 billion a year were given to the states, the states
could fund programs for education, job training, economic development, social and health services, housing,
and transportation. She favors taxes on consumption,
which are hard to evade. Drug dealers and gamblers are
unlikely to pay income taxes, but they are all consumers.
Not all functions of government need to flow from Washington. In many cases, the states could spend the money
more efficiently.

One task that only Washington can accomplish is to slow
down the rate of increase in federal entitlement programs.
Social security, Medicaid for the elderly, and Medicare for
the poor, along with other pension programs, make up the
largest and fastest-growing component of the federal budget. The United States spends more on entitlement programs than it spends on defense or in interest on the
national debt. Some of these benefits, including the biggest, social security, are tied to the cost of living; when the
Consumer Price Index goes up, as it always does, the
benefits increase accordingly. As the American population
grows older (the median age may reach forty-five in the
early twenty-first century; it is now thirty-two), these programs, unless checked, will overwhelm all other responsibilities of government and produce insupportable deficits.
It is not a new problem. When he was in the White

House, Richard Nixon endorsed the idea of increasing benefits as the cost of living went up; Nixon later said that this change had been his gravest fiscal mistake as president.

Entitlements have been woven into the fabric of American life. Here is how Peter G. Peterson, former secretary of commerce, described them in his book, *On Borrowed Time:*

> It appears that everyone today, rich or poor, is entitled to something—from the elderly, who are "entitled" to more tax-free Social Security benefits than they have earned and more health care than they need; to veterans, who are, among numerous other things, "entitled" to free health care whether or not their disabilities are service-related; to farmers and ranchers, who, in good times or bad, are "entitled" to income-transfer payments, subsidized electric power, cheap water, and free grazing rights; to public service employees, some of whom are "entitled" in retirement to more income than they ever earned in government service; and—yes, you guessed it—to Peter G. Peterson, whose simple citizenship "entitles" him to a panoply of tax-free government benefits upon his retirement, regardless of his financial need and regardless of whether he has paid for them.

The words of an angry citizen, and an accurate description of the middle-class welfare state in which we live.

Most of the money goes to Americans over age sixty-five, who make up only 12 percent of the population. Americans think of the elderly as poor or destitute. They are not. By nearly every measurement, the elderly are better off than any other age group. But there are 37 million people over age sixty-five, and they constitute an organized, well-financed, and powerful political lobby that is determined to hold on to what it gets from the government. What it gets is a lot of money. As we have seen, for every dollar the U.S. government spends on Americans under age eighteen, it spends eleven dollars on Americans over age sixty-five.

The solution to this problem is simple: Give social security to those who need it, and give less of it to those who don't. It is not true that Americans over sixty-five are the poorest group in the society, although many believe that. There is incontestable evidence that the old are better off then any other age group. After taxes, including state, local, and property taxes, elderly Americans have more income than the nonelderly. There are poor and destitute old Americans, but most are relatively well off. The war on poverty among the aged was won a number of years ago. Most people on social security today can afford to pay higher taxes on their benefits or accept a reduction in their cost-of-living benefit increases. These savings could be made without hurting those who are poor, and in fact would increase the money available to help those who need help the most.

There is no test of income or assets applied to those who receive social security or Medicare; the rich and the middle class get it automatically along with the poor. People who apply for Medicaid or food stamps, however, must prove that they need the government's help. If the poor can be tested, why not the well-off? Some of the elderly reply that because they and their employers paid social security taxes for years, the money belongs to them. It does, but not as much as they're getting. Social security payments have little relation to what was contributed over a worker's lifetime. If social security checks were calculated only on the contributions of recipients and their employers, in amounts adjusted for inflation, the checks would be much smaller. Paying back only what was put in, adjusted for inflation, would save many billions of dollars every year.

That is not what is proposed, and it would be unfair. What would be fair would be a reduction in benefits for those who don't need them, and no reduction for those who depend on them. The elderly poor would get what they're getting now, and the rest of the elderly would get a little less. Not finding some way to slow down the locomotive of entitlements will lead the country into certain disaster only a few years from now.

Further, the idea that sixty-five is the proper retirement age is artificial. It was, in fact, the result of a con game operated by Otto von Bismarck, the chancellor of Germany, in 1889. There was agitation in Germany at that time for a pension system for retired workers. Bismarck reluctantly agreed, but he set the retirement age at seventy. That was the con game: Workers in Germany in 1889 had a life expectancy of *forty-five years*. Under Bismarck's plan, no one would be alive to collect a government pension. The retirement age was later lowered to sixty-five, and that's where it stands today, a century later. It remains an artificial standard, made even less meaningful by the longer life expectancy of Americans today.

When social security was enacted in the 1930s, 25 percent of the population lived on farms. Today, that proportion has dropped to 2 percent. Yet the school year in the United States remains tied to a pastoral, agricultural America that needed children to help with crops in the summer and chores in the afternoon. A school year that runs from September to June is an anachronism in today's world. Among all the proposals made to repair and re-build America's tattered educational system, the most intriguing is that primary and secondary schools be kept open all year. Ernest L. Boyer, president of the Carnegie Foundation for the Advancement of Teaching, wants to change the academic calendar and let the schools run for twelve months instead of nine, with appropriate holiday vacations but no long summer vacation. Roughly speak-ing, that would increase the time for study by about one-fourth. If Johnny is having trouble reading on a nine-month schedule, might we not expect him to be more proficient if he had 25 percent more time for his studies? No one claims that a full-year school schedule would improve the performance of American students by 25 per-cent. If that could be guaranteed, we should do it tomor-row morning. But it is reasonable to expect that year-round schooling would improve American education significantly.

Dr. Boyer also points out that schools now waste valu-able time in the afternoons. That time could be put to better use in additional educational programs, and, even more important, for preschool education. It might also solve some day-care problems for working parents. And it would establish the neighborhood school as a full-time, year-round institution. In inner cities, the school and the church are the only stable, permanent institutions. In many areas, the schools provide the only hot, nourishing meal that a child gets that day. A changed schedule would provide additional educational nourishment as well. It would raise the cost of education, but it might very well be worth the price. If the United States is unable to train an educated work force for the next century, all other reforms will be meaningless.

It is likely that the American armed forces will be smaller in the next century. If the Soviet Union brings down the size of its military establishment so that it no longer is a military threat to Western Europe, the United States will be able to scale down and spend less on defense. The armed services would have less need for recruitment. Is this, therefore, the time to consider some form of national service for young men and women?

There are many tasks that could be set before a national service corps. The country's bridges and roads need repairing. Bad housing needs restoration. The poor and disadvantaged need help, especially after the cutbacks in social services during the Reagan years. Some young people could teach others, which would be a boon to the educational system. Some could serve in inner cities, rebuilding abandoned housing. A national service corps would provide a drug-free environment, at least to the degree to which that could be controlled. It would mix rich and poor, urban and suburban, young people of all races and cultures. Too many poor youngsters in the cities today have grown up in conditions of anarchy and lawlessness; two years of disciplined and purposeful service could change their attitude toward life, and the experience could do no harm to children of the suburbs. President Bush has a plan called YES, Youth Entering Service, and a number of proposals for national service have been made by Democrats in the Congress.

In 1995, there will be something like 2 million eighteen-year-old men and women. Sixteen million Americans served together in World War II. Most of them emerged from that experience more tolerant of their fellow Americans and more understanding of people unlike themselves. A national service corps would duplicate some of those wartime relationships, and the people in it would learn the meaning of working together on useful projects. A more cooperative spirit is needed in this country after the self-centered years of the 1980s.

America is not *at* war today, but it is *in* a war with its competitors overseas, with the Japanese and the Europeans, with other countries on the Pacific Rim. One way of winning that war, one of the things that Americans need to do, is to stop thinking of the Japanese as super-people. The question has been asked, "Should we become more like the Japanese?" In some ways we should. The Japanese, with a population half our size, have spent three times as much on new plants and equipment than we have in the past fifteen years; they spend more on civilian research and development and far more on new bridges, roads, and transportation systems than we do; they save a lot more; and they educate their young better. But these are not mysterious oriental accomplishments. They are the building blocks of any industrial society anywhere. And a great deal of what the Japanese know they learned from us. We taught them much of what they know about building a contemporary industrial system.

Many of their most successful commercial products were invented in the United States. American engineers taught them about modern production techniques. American scholars, during the post–World War II occupation, wrote their constitution and tutored them on liberal democracy. Should we become more like the Japanese? The fact is, the Japanese have become more like us. Or, more accurately, what we ought to be.

Yet we can learn from the Japanese experience in the most critical field of all: the development and sustenance of high technology through a partnership of industry and government. Technology is transforming the world. We are moving from the industrial age to the information age, and moving very quickly. As Rupert Murdoch, owner of a worldwide media empire, said, "A golden age will come to those countries which turn this wealth of information into knowledge effectively. In future, the ascendant nations with the highest living standards will be those which master not land and material but ideas and technologies." The United States still holds its lead, but the lead is slipping. It will be lost unless Americans can forge a better link between the resources of government and the resources of technology.

Not a new link, a better link. Government support for technology goes back to the earliest days of the republic. In 1806, the U.S. Congress, at the urging of Henry Clay, authorized the National Road, the new technology of its time, across the Appalachian Mountains. In 1817, New York State decided to construct the Erie Canal, another technology project. The locomotive was invented in England, but when advanced railway technology reached the United States, the government in Washington supported the expansion of the nation's railroads with gifts of public lands and loans from the U.S. Treasury.

Abram S. Hewitt, the great American ironmaster, once wrote in the early twentieth century, "The consumption of iron is the social barometer by which to estimate the relative height of civilization among nations." Today, he would write that the production of chips and computers and the processing of information are ways to estimate the height of a civilization. In 1920, the United States led the world in iron and steel manufacturing. The discovery of new sources of iron and the invention of new, high-technology methods of turning it into steel helped make the United States the world leader—but that achievement also required an indirect government subsidy in the form of a prohibitive tariff.

There are those in Washington who say that an industrial policy under which the government would assist the development of high technology would be wrong. They prefer to depend on market forces and believe that, in the long run, the market knows best. They say the government should not be in the business of picking winners and losers. But, as we have seen, the U.S. government has always picked winners and losers. It supports promising undertakings in science through government grants. Its system of taxation has supported winners through tax breaks and tax shelters. Its farm-subsidy programs, from 1986 through 1989, spent $600,000 *per farmer*. Its entitlement programs make the elderly winners and children losers.

We don't need an industrial policy. We need a technology policy to keep America competitive. Technology is America's new National Road, its Erie Canal, its railroad system, its big-steel industry. Japan's government helped its high-technology industries until they were securely on their feet; they need much less help today because they became giants with government assistance. The size of the job in the United States is beyond the resources of any individual company, and it is made more difficult by the deadly American obsession with short-term profits to keep stock prices high. There are many things the federal government can do: it can ease regulatory restrictions; it can find a way to develop cooperative partnerships by relaxing antitrust laws; it can assist sectors of American high technology that are threatened by the mercantilist practices of foreign countries. The United States spent countless billions of dollars defending its national security in a political cold war that it won. It must now spend billions defending its national security in a technological cold war—that it is losing.

There might be less opposition to these moves if there were more information about the new technology available to the people in Washington who run the government. Technology today is moving so quickly, creating so many new economic and international relations, that many of our politicians don't understand what's taking place. How much do the president or senior members of Congress actually know about things like microprocessors, photonics, numerically controlled tools, X-ray lithography, or the other entries in the dictionary of new technology? These are no longer arcane scientific topics; they are the prime agents of change in today's world. Who understands them most and uses them best will control the future. Our politicians must become technologically literate, and so must we.

■ ■ ■

We must also, above all, learn to dream again. As the decade of the 1990s begins, millions of people are dreaming of better and more productive lives. East Europeans dream of freedom, West Europeans dream of unity. Millions of Asians dream of a new and more prosperous world, and those dreams have not ended in China.

Where is our dream? Where is America's vision of the future? Americans have always been the world's greatest dreamers. We dreamed of independence, and got it. We dreamed of becoming a continental power, and accomplished it. Our immigrants dreamed of a decent and prosperous life, and won it. We dreamed of going to the moon, and got there.

Now we must dream again in a world transformed by technology and education, and we must adapt to that world. We must move beyond the comfortable distractions of the recent past and the soft illusions of the present into the hard realities of the next century. And we can do it because we have done it before. There is great peril facing the United States, but the promise of the future is even greater. All we have to do is act on what we know.

SOURCES

I am grateful to the Associated Press, which casts the widest net in the news business. The *New York Times*, the *Wall Street Journal*, *Business Week*, and *The Economist* were especially valuable in their coverage of high technology. The editorial pages of the *Washington Post* and the *Boston Globe* offered opinions and analyses that stretched my mind. The *Statistical Abstracts of the United States* was invaluable. There was much information in the papers of the House Committee on Ways and Means.

In 1987 *Congressional Quarterly* published a series of guidebooks to American politics: *Presidential Elections Since 1789*, *National Party Conventions 1831–1984*, and *Race for the Presidency*. The best journalistic account of the 1984 election was Jack W. Germond and Jules Witcover's *Wake Us When It's Over*, published by Macmillan in 1985. The Germond-Witcover account of the 1988 presidential election, *Whose Broad Stripes and Bright Stars*, published by Warner Books in 1989, was the most insightful book on that contest.

I found Paul Kennedy's *The Rise and Fall of the Great Powers* (Vintage Books, 1989) stimulating and informative. Equally useful were several Adelphi papers written for the International Institute for Strategic Studies in the spring of 1989, especially one by Professor Samuel Huntington of Harvard.

Among the volumes on economics that helped me were Robert Heilbroner and Peter Bernstein's tightly argued *The Debt and the Deficit* (Norton, 1989); Benjamin M. Friedman's

Day of Reckoning (Random House, 1988); and an extremely useful book called *The Global Economy*, edited by Robert D. Hormats and William E. Brock for the American Assembly (Norton, 1990). And anyone who wants to enter the thicket of government entitlement programs should be guided by Peter G. Peterson and Neil Howe's *On Borrowed Time* (ICS Press, 1988).

Arthur T. Hadley's *The Straw Giant* (Random House, 1986) contains a compelling description of the failed hostage rescue mission in Iran during the Carter administration, and President Carter's own memoir, *Keeping Faith* (Bantam, 1982), offers more details. Robert Graham's *Iran—The Illusion of Power* (St. Martin's Press, 1979) is an outstanding piece of work on pre-Khomeini Iran.

The Reagan presidency produced a flood of books about the White House, and among the most interesting are Laurence I. Barret's *Gambling with History* (Doubleday, 1983) and *The Reagan Legacy*, edited by Sidney Blumenthal and Thomas Byrne Edsall (Pantheon Books, 1988). *Perspectives on the Reagan Years*, edited by John L. Palmer (Urban Institute Press, 1986), is another in a series of commentaries on government that makes the Urban Institute so uniquely valuable.

The *American Agenda* report to President Bush, compiled under the sponsorship of former presidents Ford and Carter, is to my mind the clearest outline of the problems facing the United States and the best collection of ideas on how they can be solved. This outstanding piece of work was put together under the direction of James M. Cannon and Stuart E. Eizenstat.

Nobody writes about Japan without first reading James Fallows of the *Atlantic*, and in addition to his magazine journalism I learned much from his *More Like Us* (Houghton Mifflin, 1989). Clyde V. Prestowitz, Jr., presents a chilling account of Japanese-American rivalry in *Trading Places* (Basic Books, 1988). *Made in America* by the MIT Commission on Industrial

Productivity (MIT Press, 1989) was very helpful. Perhaps most stimulating of all that I read about our relationship with Japan was David Halberstam's majestic *The Reckoning* (Morrow, 1986).

So many people assisted me in other ways that it would take too much space to list them here, but I owe a debt of thanks to Joyce Thompson, whose careful and able research was of great help.

INDEX

ABC, 77, 84, 85
Afghanistan, Soviet invasion of, 85, 104
Agnew, Spiro, 63, 65–66, 67
agrobusiness, 24
Ailes, Roger, 141
Alexander, Lamar, 48
All the President's Men, 75
American Agenda, 151
American Electronics Association, 28, 39
American Medical Association, 143
Ampex, 74
antitrust laws, 32, 40
Apollo XVII, 59
Apple Computer, 40
ARCO Solar, 36
Armstrong, Neil, 59
AT&T, 40
automobile industry, 21, 71–73

baby boomers, 113–114
Baker, Howard, 95
Baker, James Addison, III, 100–102
Bell Canada, 42
Bismarck, Otto von, 156
blacks, poverty and, 51–52
Boesky, Ivan, 113
Boskin, Michael, 45
Boston harbor, pollution of, 18, 136
Bottoms, Robert, 46, 47
Bowsher, Charles A., 121, 122, 124
Boyer, Ernest L., 157
Brady, Nicholas, 125

Brezhnev, Leonid, 86
Bromley, D. Allan, 31
Brown, Harold, 150
Bush, George, 31, 36, 38, 80, 101, 121, 122, 150, 151
    Congressional reform proposal of, 148
    costs inherited by, 124–125
    HDTV and, 41–42
    1988 presidential campaign of, 18, 136, 138, 141
    Panama and, 90
    Reagan and, 94–95
    YES plan of, 158
business-government partnerships, 31–32, 34, 40, 41–42, 160–162

Caddell, Patrick, 77
Calhoun, John, 63
Califano, Joseph, 78–79
Camp David Accords, 93
Canada, 42, 48, 49, 85
Canon, 44
Carnegie Foundation for the Advancement of Teaching, 157
Carter, Jimmy, 74–80, 92–93, 96, 103, 132, 133, 150, 151
    anti-Washington campaign of, 75, 94
    Iran and, 80, 81, 82, 86–89, 90, 102
    national morale and, 77–80, 87, 89, 90, 100, 113, 142
    SALT II treaty and, 85–86
Cavazos, Lauro F., 49

CBS, 84, 85, 120
Census Bureau, U.S., 52
Center for Educational
    Research, 49
Center for Political Studies,
    119–120
Central Intelligence Agency
    (CIA), 16, 66, 86, 88
Cheney, Richard, 146
Chicago Tribune, 112
children, poverty and, 52–54
Children's Defense Fund, 52
China, 163
    Nixon and, 69, 93
Clay, Henry, 160
Common Cause, 148, 149
Compaq Computer, 28
computer industry, 25–27, 42,
    160
    declining U.S. share of,
        25–27, 28, 29–32
    dynamic random access
        memory (D-RAM) chips
        and, 30, 34
    federal government and, 27
    of Japan, 25–27, 30
    laptops in, 28
    minisupercomputers in, 26
    semiconductors in, 29–32,
        39
    supercomputers in, 25–27
Confucius, 66
Congress, U.S., 34, 67, 69, 93,
    95, 97, 109, 110, 141,
    142–150, 160
    cost of, 144–147
    Democratic control of, 96,
        104, 105, 108, 123, 146
    incumbency and, 135, 145,
        147–148
    public's view of, 142–144
    reform of, 147–150
conservatism vs. liberalism,
    132–135
Constitution, U.S., 64, 93, 136,
    145, 150
consumer electronics industry,
    21
    declining U.S. share of,
        27–29, 73–74

of Japan, 28, 29, 73–74
    size of, 27
Contras, *see* Iran-Contra
    scandals
Control Data, 26
corporations, management and
    profit philosophies of, 71
Council on Competitiveness, 48
Cranston, Alan, 145–146
Cray, Seymour R., 26
Cray Research, 26–27
Cuba, Grenada and, 116–117

Dart, Justin, 101
Dean, John, 64
Deaver, Michael, 101, 102
Defense Department, U.S., 30,
    31, 41, 44, 86–87, 90, 117,
    122, 124, 146–147
defense research and
    development (R & D) 44
Defense Science Board, 29–30
Democratic party, 75, 100, 109,
    114, 120, 159
    bipartisanship proposed for,
        134–135, 150
    Congress controlled by, 96,
        104, 105, 108, 123, 146
    image of, 67
    liberalism and, 132, 133
    Reagan and, 94, 95, 103
Depression, Great, 54, 97, 132,
    133
Dewey, Thomas E., 141
Double Income, No Kids
    (DINKS), 112
Dukakis, Michael, 18, 136, 138
dynamic random access
    memory (D-RAM) chips,
    30, 34
"Dynasty," 111

Eastern Europe, political
    changes in, 125, 130, 163
Eastwood, Clint, 109
Economist, 152
education, 46–51
    cost of, 50–51
    crisis state of, 16, 24, 48–50,
        130

science, 46–48
year-round, 157–158
Education Department, U.S.,
47–48, 108
Egypt, 93
Eisenhower, Dwight D., 75, 91,
121, 132, 141
election of 1980, 94, 95
election of 1988, 18, 136
electronics, see consumer
electronics industry
El Salvador, 116
"Energy and National Goals,"
(Carter), 78
engineering schools, 47
entitlement programs, cost of,
153–156, 161
environmental issues, 122, 123,
124
Erie Canal, 160
European Community, 130,
131, 162
economy of, 20–21, 28
fusion research of, 38
HDTV industry of, 40
semiconductor industry of,
32
Exxon, 36

farm-price support program,
107, 161
Federal Highway
Administration, 124–125
Federal Reserve System, 97,
151–152
Ferguson, Charles, 31
Ford, Gerald, 63, 64, 67–68,
70, 74–75, 91, 93, 96, 142,
151
foreign aid, 125
France, 28
Fujitsu, 27
fusion power, 37–38

Gallup polls, 77, 100, 119
gasoline prices, 72, 76
General Accounting Office
(GAO), 121–123, 124
General Electric, 44

Germany, Federal Republic of
(West Germany), 72, 89
automobile industry of, 73
economic production by, 16
exports by, 17–18
income tax in, 152
Mag-Lev trains of, 33–35
poverty in, 53
R & D spending of, 45
solar energy in, 36–37
Ghotbsadeh, Sadegh, 84
GI Bill, 114
glasnost, 131
Goldberger, Paul, 115
Goldwater, Barry, 99, 141
Gorbachev, Mikhail, 103
government-business
partnerships, 31–32, 34,
40, 41–42, 160–162
Graduate, The, 38
Graham, Robert, 81
Gramm-Rudman-Hollings Act,
147
Great Britain, 38, 48, 65, 89
corporate ownership by, in
U.S., 19
Greenspan, Alan, 151–152
Gregorian, Vartan, 50
Grenada, U.S. invasion of, 90,
116–117, 118

Hadley, Arthur T., 88
"Hail to the Chief," 65
Hamilton, Lee, 125
Harding, Warren, 64, 119
Harris surveys, 17, 77, 112,
131
Hart, Gary, 138
Heclo, Hugh, 114–115, 119
Heritage Foundation, 146
Hewitt, Abram S., 161
Hewlett-Packard, 30, 40
high-definition television
(HDTV), 28, 39–42
European Community and,
40
federal government and,
40–42
Japan and, 40
Hitachi, 26, 27, 44, 73

Hoffman, Dustin, 38
Hollings, Ernest, 29, 147
Hong Kong, 42
Hoover, Herbert, 74, 91
House Judiciary Committee, 64
House of Lords (Great Britain), 145
House of Representatives, U.S., 64, 95, 108, 123, 144, 148
House Ways and Means Committee, 144
housing:
  racism and, 52
  rising cost of, 112–113
Housing and Urban Development Department (HUD), U.S., 146
Howe, Neil, 53
Hungary, 125

IBM, 30, 40
"Immaculate Conception" process, 135
inflation, 62, 69, 70, 74, 76, 79, 90, 97, 98, 100, 112, 113, 114
Information Age, 42, 43
Institute for Social Research, 67
interest rates, 26, 45, 69, 76, 79, 90, 97, 100, 113
Interior Department, U.S., 122
Iowa, U.S.S., 90
Iran, 80–89
  under shah, 80–83, 84
  U.S. hostages in, 83–89, 90, 100, 102, 113, 114
Iran: The Illusion of Power (Graham), 81
Iran-Contra scandals, 80, 104, 120
Ishihara, Shintaro, 20, 32
Israel, 35, 61, 89, 93
Italy, 89
Iverson, J. Richard, 28

Jack Murphy Stadium, 112
Jackson, Andrew, 63
Japan:
  assets of, 54

automobile industry of, 21, 71–73
computer industry of, 25–27, 30
consumer electronics industry of, 28, 29, 73–74
culture of, 70
economy of, 16, 18, 19
education in, 49
foreign aid by, 125
government support of industry in, 162
HDTV industry of, 40
income tax in, 152
lack of poverty and racism in, 52
lessening competition from, 130–131
Mag-Lev trains of, 33–35
public perception of world economic standing of, 17
R & D spending of, 45
savings rate of, 70
solar energy in, 36–37
telecommunications investment by, 43
U.S. relations with, 20, 39, 130–131, 159–160
during World War II, 20
Japan That Can Say No, The (Morita/Ishihara), 19–20, 32
Jefferson, Thomas, 68
Johnson, Lyndon B., 91, 93, 141
Jorgensen, Earl, 101
Justice Department, U.S., 64, 124

Kelly, Walt, 79
Kennedy, Edward, 77, 79
Kennedy, John F., 91, 113, 141–142
Kennedy, Paul, 12
Kent State student killings, 62
Khomeini, Ayatollah Ruhollah, 82, 84
Kirkpatrick, Jeane, 137
Kissinger, Henry, 83, 93

Korea, Republic of (South
    Korea), 20, 48
  computer industry of, 30
  students from, in U.S., 47
Korean War, 63

Labor Department of, U.S., 108
Landon, Alf, 69
laptop computers, 28
Lebanon, 90
  U.S. hostages in, 80
  U.S. marines killed in,
    105–106, 107
liberalism vs. conservatism,
    132–135
Los Angeles, 111

McGovern, George, 69
Magaziner, Ira, 28
Markey, Edward J., 40
Massachusetts, prison furlough
    program of, 18, 136
MasterCard, 42
Matsushita Electric, 28
Medicaid, 153, 155
Medicare, 133, 153, 155
Meese, Edwin, III, 100, 101,
    102
Mexico, 49
minisupercomputers, 26
Mitsubishi, 19, 73
Mohammed Reza Shah Pahlavi,
    61, 80–83, 84
Mondale, Walter, 103, 106,
    136
money worship, 110–113
Morita, Akio, 19–20
Motorola, 36
Moynihan, Daniel Patrick, 34
Murdoch, Rupert, 160

Nader, Ralph, 149
NASA, 44, 59
National Assessment of
    Educational Progress, 48
National Commission on
    Excellence in Education,
    49
National Geographic Society,
    48

National Research Council, 38,
    51
National Road, 160
national service corps, 158
NBC News, polls by, 17, 19
  "NBC Nightly News," 84
NEC, 27
New Deal, 75, 98, 132
New York Times, 28, 31, 45, 115,
    120, 121
Nicaragua, 116
Nihon Keizai Shimbun, 54
Nixon, Richard, 61, 63, 68,
    119, 132, 141, 142, 154
  shah of Iran and, 80–81
  Watergate and, 64–66, 67,
    69, 74–75, 77, 91, 93, 133
Norris, Chuck, 116

oil crisis of 1970s, 61–62, 70,
    72, 74, 76, 79, 80, 81, 103
Olympic Games (1980), 85, 117
Olympic Games (1984),
    117–118
Olympic Games (1992), 40
On Borrowed Time (Peterson and
    Howe), 53, 154
Organization of Petroleum
    Exporting Countries
    (OPEC), 61, 62, 70, 72, 74,
    76, 80, 71, 103

Panama, U.S. invasion of, 90
Patent Office, U.S., 44
patriotism, profit in, 116
Pearl Harbor, attack on, 22
pension programs, 153
Pentagon Papers, The, 66
perestroika, 131
Peterson, Peter G., 53, 154
Philips, 32
Pledge of Allegiance, 18
Poland, 125
political action committees
    (PACs), 148
Porter, Roger, 41
poverty, 24, 51–54, 60, 110,
    120, 130
  blacks and, 51–52
  children of, 52–54

presidency, diminished
confidence in, 65–66, 67,
69, 74, 77, 78, 91–93, 104
presidential campaign reform,
135–141
President's Council of
Economic Advisors, 45
Princeton University, fusion
research at, 38
productivity, 61, 71, 78
Proposition, 13, 75
"public realm," 115–116

Qaddafi, Muammar al-, 90

racism, 51–52
Ranney, Austin, 137, 138
Rather, Dan, 85
Reagan, Nancy, 120
Reagan, Ronald, 79, 86, 93,
94–110, 114, 132, 133, 142
budget cuts by, 95, 108
defense spending of, 44, 96,
97, 108, 120
election of, 90–91, 94, 136
GAO report on, 121–123
Grenada and, 116, 117, 118
image of, 103–107
Iran and, 80, 102, 104, 120
Lebanon Marine massacre
and, 105–106, 107
as professional politician,
107–108, 120
public opinion of, 119–121
taxes and, 95, 96–97, 108
timidity of, 99
as U.S. booster, 18, 94, 98,
100, 118
vision of, 94
White House staff of,
100–102
recession of 1981–1982, 76,
97–98, 104, 110, 113, 114
recessions, 108–109
Regan, Donald, 102
Republican party, 96, 97, 109,
118, 146
bipartisanship proposed for,
134–135, 150, 151

conservatism and, 133
deregulation and, 114
New Deal and, 132
Reagan and, 94–95, 119
research and development (R &
D), 43–45, 71
Ribicoff, Abraham, 151
Rise and Fall of the Great Powers,
The (Kennedy), 12
Rivlin, Alice M., 152–153
Robertson, Pat, 136
Rockefeller, David, 83
Rockefeller Center, Mitsubishi's
purchase of, 19
Roosevelt, Franklin D., 69, 75,
91, 98, 103, 132, 151
Roosevelt, Theodore, 92
Rostenkowski, Dan, 144–145
Royko, Mike, 112
Rudman, Warren B., 147
"Ruffles and Flourishes," 65

SALT II treaty, 85–86
San Diego Padres, 112
savings and loan institutions (S
& L), federal bail-out of,
124, 146
savings rates, 66, 70, 76, 79,
110
Sawyer, David, 103
Schlesinger, Arthur M., Jr.,
119
Schulberg, Budd, 110
Schurz, Carl, 11
scientists, U.S., decline in,
46–48
Screen Actors' Guild, 103
Sematech, 31
semiconductor industry, 29–32,
39
Senate, U.S., 85–86, 104, 105,
123, 144, 145, 148
Senate Committee on Public
Works, 34
Senate Watergate Committee,
64
SGS-Thompson, 32
shah of Iran, 61, 80–83, 84
Shell, 36
Shultz, George, 104

Siemens, A.G., 32, 36
Singapore, 20, 42
Smith, Adam, 66
Smith, William French, 101
social security, 97, 100, 107,
    133, 153–156
solar energy, economics of,
    35–37
Sony, 19, 40, 73
Soviet Union:
  Afghanistan invaded by, 85,
    104
  U.S. and, 69, 93, 96, 98, 103,
    104–105, 117–118, 120,
    25, 129, 131, 158
Sputnik, 22
Stallone, Sylvester, 116
State Department, U.S., 122
Stevenson, Adlai, 141
Straw Giant, The (Hadley),
    88–89
supercomputers, 25–27
Supreme Court, U.S., 147
sushi, 112
Sweden, poverty in, 53

Taiwan, 20
tax cheating, 111
taxes, raising of, 151–153
taxpayers' rebellions, 75
Teapot Dome scandal, 64–65
telecommunications, 42–43
television, political conventions
    covered by, 140
Toshiba, 44
Tower, John, 144
trains, Mag-Lev, 33–35
Transportation Department,
    U.S., 34, 122
transportation technology, 24,
    33–35
Truman, Harry S, 91, 103, 132,
    141
Tsipis, Kostas, 45
Tuttle, Holmes, 101
Twain, Mark, 143

unemployment, 60, 70, 90, 97,
    98, 108, 114

United States:
  assets of, 54
  defense spending of, 44, 96,
    97, 108, 120, 158
  federal deficit of, 16, 96, 87,
    98, 99, 108–109, 129, 151,
    152
  foreign capital in, 16, 70,
    109, 110
  foreign corporate ownership
    in, 19, 23, 25
  foreign debt of, 22, 23, 25,
    97, 109, 129
  foreign students in, 47
  inventions of, developed
    elsewhere, 21, 30, 33, 40
  Iran and, 61, 80–89, 90, 100,
    102, 113, 114
  as jungle or zoo, 132–135
  as leading producer, 16, 21,
    54, 60, 115, 160
  national morale of, 64,
    66–67, 72, 73, 74, 77,
    78–79, 83, 85, 87, 89, 90,
    98, 100, 113, 142
  Panama invaded by, 90
  post-Vietnam military
    operations of, 89–90
  private debt in, 22, 60, 76,
    108–109, 110, 116
  standard of living of, 16, 18,
    19, 22, 60, 70, 71, 76,
    79–80, 114
  trade deficit of, 16, 23, 60,
    129–130
  waning public confidence in,
    17, 18–19
  as world leader, 125–126,
    129–135
Urban Institute, 53
urban underclass, 24
U.S. Memories, 30–31
Utah University, fusion
    research at, 37

Vance, Cyrus, 86, 89, 150–151
Vander Jagt, Guy, 145
Veterans Affairs Department,
    U.S., 108
Vietnam War, 59–60, 62–63,

Vietnam War *(cont.)*
66–67, 91, 93, 100, 113,
114
Visa, 42
Volcker, Paul, 97, 152

wages, 112
Walkman, 19
Wallace, George, 67
Wall Street Journal, 17, 19, 47,
149
Washington Post, 104
Watergate scandal, 64–65,
65–66, 67, 69, 74–75, 77,
91, 93, 133
Well-off Old People
(WHOOPIES), 112
Western Europe, *see* European
Community
What Makes Sammy Run?
(Schulberg), 110–111

wheat, sales of, to Soviet
Union, 85, 104–105
White, Theodore H., 136
White House Budget Office,
124
Will, George, 106, 120
Wills, Garry, 102
Wilson, Pete, 149
WIN campaign, 70
women, labor force and, 76–77,
114
Wright, Jim, 143

Yankelovich, Daniel, 98
Yom Kippur War, 61, 62
Youth Entering Service (YES)
plan, 158
Yuppies, 112, 113

Zenith, 28–29